Examining The Pre-Wrath Rapture of the Church

Marvin Rosenthal
Kevin Howard

THOMAS NELSON PUBLISHERS
Nashville

Previously published by Zion's Hope Inc.

Published in Nashville, Tennessee, by Thomas Nelson, Inc., Publishers, and distributed in Canada by Word Communications, Ltd., Richmond, British Columbia, and in the United Kingdom by Word (UK), Ltd., Milton Keynes, England.

Scripture quotations are from The Holy Bible, KING JAMES VERSION.

Printed in the United States of America

1 2 3 4 5 6 7 8 — 00 99 98 97 96 95 94

ISBN 0-7852-8167-3

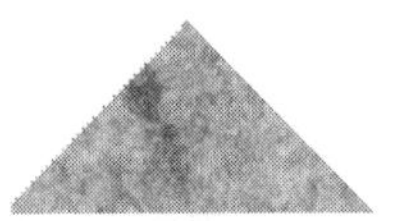

To all those who keep the commandments of God and have the testimony of Jesus Christ.

Revelation 12:17

Contents

THE CONTENT

A Personal Study Guide

This book has been designed as a study guide for the book, *The Prewrath Rapture of the Church.* It is written in a simplistic and structured manner for the serious student of God's Word who is interested in a biblical study of Christ's second coming.

The end goal of this study is to thoroughly understand the concepts and Scriptures surrounding Christ's second coming. To achieve that goal it is, therefore, extremely important to carefully read *all assignments* in the book, *The Prewrath Rapture of the Church,* before answering the questions in each lesson. It is also vital that *all Scripture verses* be looked up when listed for a particular question. God holds us each individually accountable to "study to show thyself approved unto God, a workman that needeth not to be ashamed, rightly dividing the word of truth" (2 Tim. 2:15). To that end, may our God richly reward your diligence in this study, and may we together with John say, "Even so, come, Lord Jesus" (Rev. 22:20).

List some specific goals that you wish to achieve by working through this study guide.

____

____

____

____

____

Introduction

Almost two thousand years ago, the **LAMB** of God **CAME** to the planet Earth to die for the sins of the world — that's paramount history. One day, perhaps soon, the **LION** is **COMING** back again to reign as King of kings — that's inviolable prophecy. For those who believe God's Word, there is no speculation about that supreme event. And a crescendo of voices which will one day arise, sarcastically proclaiming: "Where is the promise of his coming? For since the fathers fell asleep, all things continue as they were from the beginning of the creation" (2 Pet. 3:4) cannot diminish the absolute certainty of the King's coming.

Jesus is coming again and, in a world beset with indescribable suffering and entrapping quicksand around every bend in the journey of life, that certain expectation stands as a beacon of incomparable and blessed hope.

At His coming, those who have died in Christ throughout the long corridor of time will be physically resurrected, while those who are living will be raptured — both the dead in Christ and the living — to meet the Lord in the air (1 Th. 4:16-17). On that occasion, believers will become immortal, incorruptible, and be glorified. As wondrously blessed heirs of our Heavenly Father's grace, we will reflect His glory throughout the endless ages.

But when does the blessed hope of Christ's return and our glorification — which we now, through faith, await — come to fruition?

Is His coming for the Church signless and possible at any moment? Or must the Church enter the seventieth week of Daniel and confront the Antichrist before rapture? Obviously, it is natural to prefer the former — no one relishes the prospect of severe difficulties — but is it biblical? Will one generation of believers be

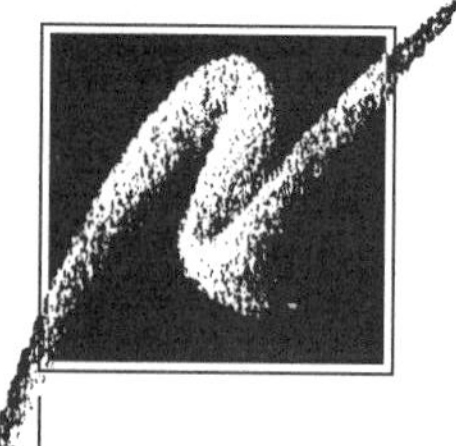

whisked to glory on beds of ease, or will that same generation be called upon to suffer persecution, or even martyrdom, for "His name's sake"? And if so, will that generation be spiritually prepared for the conflict?

Some voices have suggested that the Scriptures are *ambiguous* concerning this matter and that all views which address the chronology of Christ's return are based on inference, supposition, and innuendo — therefore, not to be pursued with vigor and seriousness of purpose.

Another group argues that consideration of the chronology of Christ's return and related events has often brought *division* and *animosity* and should be avoided.

Still others suggest that the chronology of end-time events is *not important* and so why get "worked up" over something *inconsequential.* What is important, they argue, is victorious living at the present moment.

Permit a brief observation of these views. First, the Scriptures are *not ambiguous* concerning the coming of Christ or the sequence of related events. The return of the King is one of the most important themes in Scripture — large in scope, plenteous in detail, and capable of comprehension.

Second, throughout Church history, all attempts to purify Church doctrine have been *accompanied by debate.* No believer who loves the Lord and wants to please Him desires to be *divisive.* But true unity can never be achieved if the sacrifice of truth is the price that must be paid to achieve it. There are times in life when bucking the tide and swimming upstream is the righteous, courageous, and correct path to pursue. In the end, souls who travel the high road will be commended by our Lord.

Third, seeking to understand the timing of Christ's return and the Rapture of the Church is *not simply an academic exercise.* The grave warnings and practical implications for godly living that accrue from a correct understanding of the Second Coming are not optional luxuries to be considered but **divine imperatives** to be obeyed. To disobey because of ignorance or indifference is to invite great peril.

If the Rapture is pretribulational, can happen at any moment, and is signless, that is one thing. If the Rapture is prewrath, can happen in any generation, and is preceded by the emergence of the Antichrist, that is another matter altogether.

The Bible is God's revelation to man. In a very real sense, it is a love letter. Both the words and the thoughts of the letter are divinely inspired. **Therefore, it is the Bible, not church associations, highly esteemed schools, favorite Bible teachers, or long-held traditions, which should ultimately determine what we believe concerning the Second Coming. God's Word alone should be the last arbiter — the final authority.**

This study guide has been coordinated with the book, *The Prewrath Rapture of the Church.* In large measure, the study guide is a direct response to a multitude of requests for further help by those who have read the *The Prewrath Rapture of the Church.* Together, the book and personal study guide are designed to lead the participant into an inductive self-study of what the Bible teaches concerning Christ's coming, the Rapture of the Church, the judgment of the wicked, and the practical implications these truths have for life. **This study guide is a "crisis" document. It will force those who work through it to make decisions — to move in one direction or another. In the end, passivity will not be a viable option. Action will be required.**

This study guide will not be tedious. Friends, co-workers, and Bible teachers who worked their way through it in its prepublication form (and to whom we are very grateful) found its instructions to be technically clear, its content spiritually refreshing, and its plea for holy living compelling and urgent.

The "Bereans" were noble because they "searched the scriptures daily, whether those things were so" (Acts 17:11). May we, living in these exciting and opportune days, have the courage to follow in their train.

Marv Rosenthal, Executive Director
***ZION'S** HOPE* INC.

The PreWrath Rapture:

Every Piece Falls Right Into Place.

Examining

A Personal Study Guide

THE PREWRATH RAPTURE OF THE CHURCH

Introduction to Christ's Return

Lesson Focus:
This first lesson is an introduction. In it you will look at why a discussion of Christ's return is an emotional issue for some. You will briefly study Christ's first coming and become acquainted with basic terms and concepts which deal with His return.

I. *The Tension and Anguish*

Read the Introduction and Chapter 1 of *The Prewrath Rapture of the Church* before answering the following questions.

Why is it important to understand unfulfilled prophecy? (p. xi)

Why is the Rapture question so emotional and controversial? (p. 21)

Personal Observations, Notes, or Quotes:

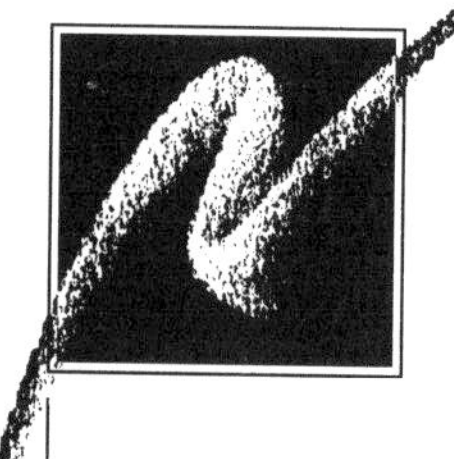

Doctrine is the great body of Bible knowledge and principles for practical Christian living of which we are commanded to "grow in grace, and in the knowledge of our Lord and Savior, Jesus Christ" (2 Pet. 3:18). What is dogma? (p. 21)

List some of the dogmas held by the Bible-believing Church. (p. 21)

What is the tendency after doctrine has been taught for years? (p. 22)

According to 2 Timothy 3:16, what is our final authority in all matters of faith and practice, the only basis for examining and modifying doctrine?

The study of Christ's second coming is part of a larger division of prophetic truth known as Eschatology. What does eschatology mean? (p. 29)

According to the book, what is the main question in an examination of the timing of the Rapture? (p. 33)

Pray that, as you diligently study with an open mind, the Lord will reveal to you the truth of His Word concerning the coming of Jesus.

Personal Observations, Notes, or Quotes:

II. *The Ultimate Absolute*

Read Chapter 2 of *The Prewrath Rapture of the Church* before answering the following questions.

According to Galatians 4:4, when did His first coming take place, and who initiated it?

Describe the divinely appointed events of the ancient world that merged together to set the stage for His first coming. (p. 38)

Why is Jesus coming again? (pp. 40-41)

What was the purpose/mission of His first coming? (p. 41)

Personal Observations, Notes, or Quotes:

Contrast His two comings in the following table. (p. 42)

1st Coming	*2nd Coming*

III. *The Options of "When" Laid Out*

Read Chapter 3 of *The Prewrath Rapture of the Church* before answering the following questions.

A. *The Millennium*

What is the meaning of the word "millennium"? (p. 46)

According to Rev. 20:1-7, what events will take place in connection with the future 1,000-year time period known as the Millennium? (p. 47)

Personal Observations, Notes, or Quotes:

What are the basic teachings of the three millennial views, and by whom and when were they begun? (pp. 48-50)

Which millennial view is held by most modern mainline Protestant denominations, and how did they come to hold such a view? (p. 50)

Why is one's view of the Millennium so important? (pp. 51-52)

In what area do all premillennialists agree concerning Christ's coming? (p. 52)

In what area do they disagree? (p. 52)

Personal Observations, Notes, or Quotes:

B. *Daniel's Seventieth Week*

Daniel was told, "Seventy weeks [literally, 'sevens'] are determined upon thy people" (Dan. 9:24). These were seventy periods of exactly seven years, or 490 years. There would be 69 sevens (483 years) from the command to rebuild Jerusalem until the coming of Messiah (Dan. 9:25). Afterwards the city of Jerusalem and the sanctuary (the temple) would be destroyed (Dan. 9:26). This was fulfilled when the Romans destroyed Jerusalem and the Temple in 70 A.D. Daniel's final seven-year period (or seventieth week) awaits the rise of a world ruler who will confirm a seven-year security agreement with Israel. Halfway through that seven-year period (3 1/2 years), he will stop the sacrifices in the rebuilt Temple and set himself up as God (Dan. 9:27; 11:31; Mt. 24:15). If the first sixty-nine weeks were literal seven-year periods, one can be absolutely certain that the seventieth week will be a literal and exact seven-year period as well.

Since the seventieth week is logically broken into two equal parts by an abomination which occurs at the midpoint, sometimes the Bible refers to the last 3 1/2 years by themselves. The biblical month was based on the moon and consisted of thirty days. Three and a half years could, therefore, be expressed as forty-two months (12 months x 3 1/2) or 1,260 days (30 days x 12 x 3 1/2) or a time, and times, and half a time (1 year + 2 years + 1/2 year).

Study the following verses and record the specific length of time in years, months, or days mentioned for Daniel's seventieth week or its last half:

Dan. 7:25

Dan. 9:27

Dan. 12:7

Rev. 11:2

Rev. 11:3

Rev. 12:6

Personal Observations, Notes, or Quotes:

Rev. 12:14

Rev. 13:5

C. *The Rapture*

What is the meaning of the word "rapture"? (p. 53)

Although the word "rapture" is not found in the English Bible, its truth is taught throughout the pages of the New Testament. What things will the Rapture of the Church accomplish according to the Bible (Jn. 14:3; 1 Cor. 15:51-53; 1 Th. 4:13-18)?

List the major views concerning the timing of the Rapture in relation to Daniel's seventieth week. (p. 53)

When and by whom was the pretribulational view originated? (pp. 53-54)

Personal Observations, Notes, or Quotes:

Define and make sure you understand imminency. (p. 54)

Which Rapture position has developed this doctrine? (p. 54)

Summarize the four major points (theses) of the book as stated in Chapter 3. (p. 60)

Summarize, in your own words, the concepts in this lesson that were new to you.

Personal Observations, Notes, or Quotes:

Personal Observations, Notes, or Quotes:

The PreWrath Rapture:

Every Piece Falls Right Into Place.

A Personal Study Guide

Examining

THE PREWRATH RAPTURE OF THE CHURCH

But First the Counterfeit

Lesson Focus:

In this lesson you will look at the rise and reign of a diabolical world ruler, the great counterfeit of the true Christ and King of kings.

Read Chapters 4 through 7 of *The Prewrath Rapture of the Church* before answering the following questions.

I. *The Antichrist*

Read the following verses and list some of the *names* and *deeds* of the wicked world ruler.

Dan. 7:8, 25

Dan. 9:27

Dan. 11:36-37

2 Th. 2:3-12

Personal Observations, Notes, or Quotes:

1 Jn. 2:18

Rev. 13:1-10

Rev. 17:12-13

Who will empower the Antichrist (Rev. 13:2, 4)?

Who is the dragon (Rev. 12:9)?

Where will Antichrist come from (Rev. 11:7)?

What will he do to the world (Mt. 24:24; 2 Th. 2:9-10)?

What will he do to the righteous (Dan. 7:21; Rev. 13:7, 15)?

Personal Observations, Notes, or Quotes:

What will he do to Jerusalem (Lk. 21:20-24; Rev. 11:2)?

How long will he do this (Rev. 11:2)?

How long will Israel flee from his face to the wilderness (Rev. 12:6, 14)?

What will he do to the sanctuary or Temple of God (Dan. 11:31)?

The holy Temple Mount in Jerusalem is located between the Mediterranean and Dead Seas. What will the Antichrist place there (Dan. 11:45)?

What will he do in relation to God (Dan. 7:25; 11:36-37; 2 Th. 2:3-4; Rev. 13:5-8)?

How long will he do this (Rev. 13:5)?

Who else does this sound like (Isa. 14:12-14; Lk. 4:6-7)?

Personal Observations, Notes, or Quotes:

II. *The Abomination*

Daniel prophesied of a future day when the Antichrist will make an image or idol. It will be so detestable, abhorrent, and loathsome that he simply referred to it as "the abomination." Where will that image be placed (Dan. 11:31; Mt. 24:15; Mk. 13:14; 2 Th. 2:3-4)?

This image will cause the Temple to become desolate, desecrated, polluted, and laid waste. What will the Antichrist do to the sacrificial system at the same time (Dan. 9:27; 11:31)?

When will this occur (Dan. 9:27)?

Of whose likeness will the image be (2 Th. 2:3-4; Rev. 13:14-15)?

III. *Signs*

What is the purpose of signs? (p. 97)

What sign did Jesus give to substantiate all the claims of His first coming? (p. 102)

Personal Observations, Notes, or Quotes:

The Lord's disciples asked about a future sign. What will it authenticate (Mt. 24:3)?

Personal Observations, Notes, or Quotes:

The PreWrath Rapture:

Every Piece Falls Right Into Place.

And What of the Tribulation Period?

Lesson Focus:
One of the most frequently used terms in any discussion concerning future events and the Rapture of the Church is the term "tribulation." In this lesson you will look at the Bible to see what it teaches concerning tribulation, the Great Tribulation, and its duration.

Read Chapter 8 of *The Prewrath Rapture of the Church* before answering the following questions.

I. *Tribulation, in General*

What is the meaning conveyed by the word "tribulation" (*thlipsis*, Strong's Exhaustive Concordance of the Bible #2347)? (p. 103)

What does the Bible say about the relationship of the believer to tribulation and affliction (*thlipsis*) in general? Are we exempt from it (Jn. 16:33; Acts 14:22; 1 Th. 3:3-4; Heb. 10:32)?

Personal Observations, Notes, or Quotes:

What did Paul tell Timothy would be true of all those who desire to live godly in Christ Jesus (2 Tim. 3:12)?

Did Paul experience affliction *(thlipsis)* in his life (Acts 20:23; Col. 1:24)?

Which churches did Paul say suffered *thlipsis*, or affliction (2 Cor. 8:1-2)?

What was the experience of the Thessalonian church in regard to affliction *(thlipsis)*, or tribulation (1 Th. 1:6)?

What was their response to this experience (2 Th. 1:4)?

What was John's common bond with the churches of Asia in relation to tribulation (Rev. 1:9)?

Does the experience of tribulation in the life of the believer mean that the Lord has broken His promises or no longer loves him (Rom. 8:35)?

Where is comfort to be found in the midst of tribulation (2 Cor. 1:3-4)?

Personal Observations, Notes, or Quotes:

What are some end results of tribulation in our lives (Rom. 5:3; 2 Cor. 4:17; 1 Th. 3:7, 13; cf. 1 Pet. 1:7; 4:12-13)?

In contrast to tribulation, what promises does the child of God possess in regard to God's wrath (Rom. 5:9; 8:1; 1 Th. 1:10; 5:9)?

Is there any doubt or uncertainty about these promises?

In light of what we have learned concerning believers and tribulation (*thlipsis*) in general, take a moment and pray for believers throughout the world who are now suffering fiery persecution for the Word of God and the testimony of Jesus Christ.

On Target

Nowhere in Scripture is the believer exempted from tribulation (persecution by this world), but instead is to expect it. However, the believer is gloriously promised the Lord's continual presence (Mt. 28:20), even in the midst of difficulties, and is promised deliverance from God's wrath.

II. *The Description of the Great Tribulation*

Why is it incorrect to refer to Daniel's seventieth week as "the tribulation period"? (p. 103)

Personal Observations, Notes, or Quotes:

What did the Lord prophesy would occur in the future (Mt. 24:9, 21; Mk. 13:19; cf. Jer. 30:6-7; Dan 12:1)?

How will this time compare to any other time of history?

What event in the Temple will initiate the Great Tribulation (Mt. 24:15-21; Mk. 13:14-19; cf. Dan. 11:31-33)?

From your earlier study, when will the abomination of desolation occur and consequently begin the Great Tribulation (Dan. 9:27)?

According to Luke, what will simultaneously befall the city of Jerusalem (Lk. 21:20-24)?

Against whom will the Great Tribulation be directed (Mt. 24:9-13, 22; Mk. 13:9-13, 20; Lk. 21:12-19; Rev. 6:9-11; 7:9-14; 12:17; 13:7, 15; 20:4)?

The phrase "great tribulation" is used one other time in Scripture. What church will experience great tribulation in this instance (Rev. 2:18, 22)?

Personal Observations, Notes, or Quotes:

Who will be the driving force behind the persecution of the Great Tribulation (Rev. 12:12-14, 17; 13:4, 7)?

Whose wrath does the Bible say that it is (Rev. 12:12, 17)?

When Antichrist invades Jerusalem to begin the Great Tribulation, there will be "wrath upon this people [Israel]" (Lk. 21:23). In light of Revelation 12, is this God's wrath or Satan's wrath which results in the Great Tribulation?

On Target

When the Lord spoke of tribulation in a prophetic context, He referred to the Great Tribulation which begins in the middle of Daniel's seventieth week — precisely 3 1/2 years into it — never the first half of it.

Based on this, to call the entire seven-year time frame "the tribulation period" is to coin a technical phrase and superimpose it upon the Scriptures, reading into the biblical text that which it does not itself declare.

III. *The Duration of the Great Tribulation*

According to Matthew 24:22 and Mark 13:20, what will happen to the Great Tribulation as far as its duration?

The word "shortened" (*koloboo,* Strong's #2856), is rendered "to amputate" by Vine's

Personal Observations, Notes, or Quotes:

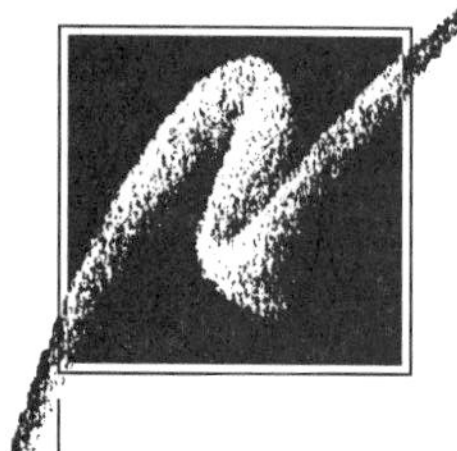

Expository Dictionary of New Testament Words. If the Great Tribulation is "amputated," will it be allowed to run the full 3 1/2 years of the last half of Daniel's seventieth week?

In light of your earlier findings regarding the length of Daniel's seventieth week in years, months, and days, what is the possibility that the last half of Daniel's seventieth week is shorter than 3 1/2 years?

What will occur immediately after the affliction of the Great Tribulation that cuts it short (Mt. 24:29; Mk. 13:24-25)?

What will the cosmic disturbance announce (Mt. 24:30; Mk. 13:26; Lk. 21:27)?

On Target

While the Bible is clear that the last half of Daniel's seventieth week is exactly 3 1/2 years or 42 months, or 1,260 days, nowhere is it taught that the Great Tribulation is the same duration. On the contrary, it is cut short, or does not continue until the end of the seventieth week. Since it begins at a different time (midpoint) than the beginning of the seventieth week, it should not be surprising if it also ends at a different point than the end of the seventieth week. Great Tribulation, by biblical definition, refers to persecution, not a 3 1/2-year period. It is the Great Tribulation (persecution) which will be cut short; not the 3 1/2-year period. The Great Tribulation will be less in duration than the final 3 1/2 years.

Personal Observations, Notes, or Quotes:

This is illustrated by the chart on page 112 of *The Prewrath Rapture of the Church*.

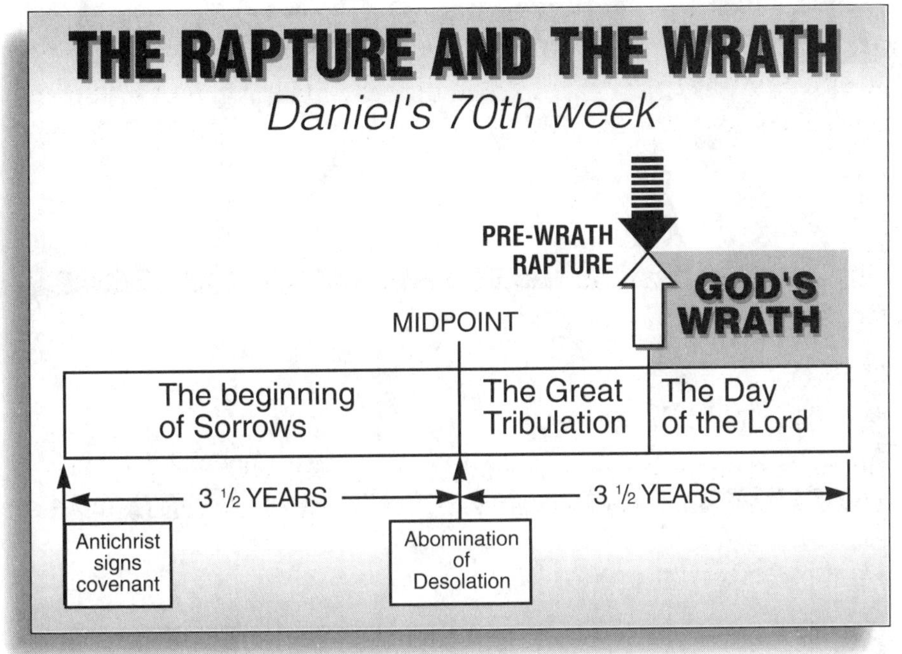

Personal Observations, Notes, or Quotes:

The PreWrath Rapture:

Every Piece Falls Right Into Place.

A Personal Study Guide

Examining

THE PREWRATH RAPTURE OF THE CHURCH

And Then the Day of the Lord

Lesson Focus:
One of the greatest errors committed in a consideration of the timing of the Rapture is the assumption that the Day of the Lord is equivalent to or starts at the beginning of Daniel's seventieth week. In this lesson you will look at the biblical passages that refer to the Day of the Lord by name and develop a description of the Day of the Lord.

Read Chapter 9 of *The Prewrath Rapture of the Church* before answering the following questions.

I. *The Description of the Day of the Lord*

Read the Day of the Lord texts and list on the following chart everything you learn about the Day of the Lord (Isa. 2:12-21; 13:6-13; 34:1-8; Ezek. 13:4-8; 30:1-3; Joel 1:15; 2:1-2, 10-11, 30-31; 3:14-16; Amos 5:18-20; Obad. 15; Zeph. 1:7-9, 14-18; 2:2-3; Zech. 14:1-2; Mal. 4:5; Acts 2:19-20; 1 Th. 5:2-4; 2 Th. 2:1-4; 2 Pet. 3:10-12).

TEXT	DESCRIPTION

Personal Observations, Notes, or Quotes:

TEXT | DESCRIPTION

II. *The Duration of the Day of the Lord*

Some commentators believe the Day of the Lord extends through the Millennium (that time of great blessing, peace, and light when the Messiah rules upon David's throne). They cite passages such as Isaiah 4:2 and Zechariah 13:1 which use the phrase "in that day" in reference to a time of blessing. They equate "in that day" with the phrase "the Day of the Lord." While it is true that a time of blessing does follow God's judgment, care must be taken to be biblical in one's definition of the Day of the Lord. The phrase "in that day" is a nonspecific time pointer which simply points to a future time period under discussion. Context must determine which future time is meant. God's judgment (the Day of the Lord) results in a subsequent time of blessing (the Millennium). The two are not synonymous. But let God's Word be the final authority.

Personal Observations, Notes, or Quotes:

From the Day of the Lord chart which you constructed from Scripture, were there any verses which spoke of blessing, peace, or light in the Day of the Lord?

Reread Amos 5:18-20, and list what elements are present and what elements are specifically excluded from the Day of the Lord.

With this clear statement of Scripture, is it possible for the Millennium to be a part of the Day of the Lord? Why?

On Target

The reason that some commentators try to include the Millennium in the Day of the Lord is that, in their prophetic framework, they believe that the present heavens and earth will be burned (2 Pet. 3:10, 12) and the new heavens and earth (2 Pet. 3:13) will be created after the Millennium instead of being restored at the beginning of it (Isa. 65:17-25). Therefore, when Peter connects the Day of the Lord to the creation of the new heavens and earth, their predetermined framework forces them to include the Millennium in the Day of the Lord. (See chart, p. 127.)

What is the context of Peter's discussion according to 2 Peter 3:4?

What will happen to the heavens and earth and to the ungodly at His coming (2 Pet. 3:7)?

Personal Observations, Notes, or Quotes:

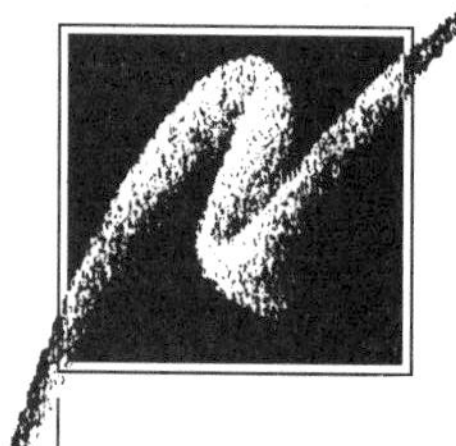

Peter described God's final judgment as one of fire as opposed to a judgment of water in the days of Noah. How does Paul describe the Lord's coming in judgment (2 Th. 1:7-8)?

Who did Isaiah say would be punished and destroyed in the Day of the Lord (Isa. 13:9, 11)?

Why does the Lord delay His coming (His promise) according to 2 Pet. 3:9?

How will the Day of the Lord come (1 Th. 5:2; 2 Pet. 3:10)?

To whom will it *not* come this way (1 Th. 5:4-9; 2 Pet. 3:11-12)?

What will be the effect of the Day of the Lord upon the heavens and the earth (2 Pet. 3:10, 12)?

What effects of the Lord's coming and presence are comparable to Peter's description in the following verses (Ps. 46:6; 97:5; Isa. 34:4, 8; 64:1-3; Amos 9:5; Mic. 1:3-4; Nah. 1:5-6; Zeph. 1:18; 3:8)?

Personal Observations, Notes, or Quotes:

Who else did Peter say had written unto his readers about the Lord's second coming and the Day of the Lord (2 Pet. 3:15-16)?

Never once did Paul describe the Day of the Lord as occurring after the millennial kingdom. If Paul's and Peter's Day of the Lord are the same, must Peter's Day of the Lord take place before or after the millennial kingdom?

How does Peter describe those teachers who try to change what he teaches concerning those future events (2 Pet. 3:16)?

Personal Observations, Notes, or Quotes:

The PreWrath Rapture:

Every Piece Falls Rig... Place.

Examining

A Personal Study Guide

THE PREWRATH RAPTURE OF THE CHURCH

Cosmic Disturbance

Lesson Focus:
The Bible often speaks of future cataclysmic turbulence in the sun, moon, and stars. In this lesson you will compare the Lord's teaching about Daniel's seventieth week with the seals of Revelation and study the connection of cosmic disturbance with the Day of the Lord.

Read Chapter 10 of *The Prewrath Rapture of the Church* before answering the following questions.

I. *The Seals of Revelation*

What are some of the arguments put forth by pretribulation rapturists to defend the premise that the Day of the Lord starts at the beginning of Daniel's seventieth week? (pp. 140-143)

A. *The Relationship of the Seals to the Olivet Discourse*

In the Book of Revelation, John saw a scroll sealed with seven seals. As the Lamb of God opened each seal, certain events occurred which prophetically described the

Personal Observations, Notes, or Quotes:

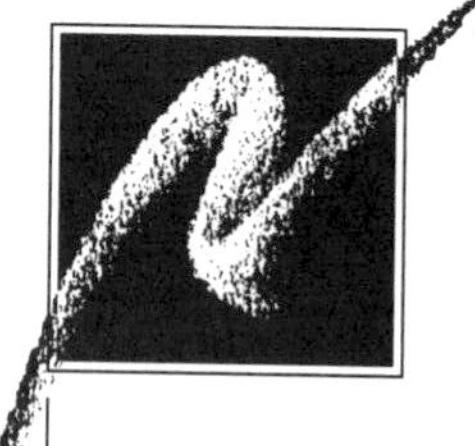

future events of Daniel's seventieth week. Describe in your own words the events of each seal.

The first seal (Rev. 6:1-2):

The second seal (Rev. 6:3-4):

The third seal (Rev. 6:5-6):

The fourth seal (Rev. 6:7-8):

The fifth seal (Rev. 6:9-11):

The sixth seal (Rev. 6:12-17):

The seventh seal (Rev. 8:1-6):

Who is the author of the Book of Revelation who revealed it unto the apostle John through an angel (Rev. 1:1; 22:16)?

Personal Observations, Notes, or Quotes:

Who gave the Olivet Discourse (Mt. 24:4)?

If the authors were the same and the topic was the same, should the two testimonies agree?

In His discourse on the Mount of Olives, Jesus described the events of Daniel's seventieth week in the exact chronological order as the seals of Revelation. Noting their parallel to the seals, what did Jesus say would be the order of events?

First event (Mt. 24:4-5; Mk. 13:5-6; Lk. 21:8):

Second event (Mt. 24:6-7a; Mk. 13:7-8a; Lk. 21:9-10):

Third event (Mt. 24:7b; Mk. 13:8c; Lk. 21:11b):

Fourth event (Mt. 24:7c; Lk. 21:11c):

Fifth event (Mt. 24:9-22; Mk. 13:9-23; Lk. 21:12-24):

Sixth event (Mt. 24:29-30; Mk. 13:24-25; Lk. 21:11d, 25-26):

What did the Lord call the first through fourth events (Mt. 24:8)?

Personal Observations, Notes, or Quotes:

What did the Lord call the fifth event (Mt. 24:21)?

What should the Lord's followers do when they see the cosmic disturbances (Lk. 21:28)?

As a result of the cosmic disturbances, what will they know is very near (Lk. 21:28)?

In light of that, until what day are believers sealed by the Holy Spirit (Eph. 4:30)?

On Target

Both Paul (1 Th. 5:2-3) and Isaiah (Isa. 13:6, 8) refer to the Day of the Lord as a woman in travail; that is, a woman in the hard, bearing-down labor of childbirth. The Lord spoke of the first four seals as the beginning of birth pangs. Birth pangs are those beginning twinges that come and go at irregular intervals as a warning that the travail is coming soon. Once the travail or bearing down (the Day of the Lord) begins, no one escapes out of it. It will not subside until it has run the full course of God's wrath upon the wicked.

B. *The Relationship of the Seals to God's Wrath*

Pretribulation rapturists usually hold that the seals are God's wrath. Does the Bible explicitly say that the first six seals are His wrath (Rev. 6)?

Personal Observations, Notes, or Quotes:

The first seal/event will be the rise of false Christs.
Does God ever sanction or promote error (Dt. 18:20; Jer. 23:29-32; 28:15-16)?

According to Isaiah 2:12 and 17, who alone will be exalted in the Day of the Lord?

The Antichrist will rise to power and exalt himself (Dan. 11:36; 2 Th. 2:4) in the middle of Daniel's seventieth week. Why would this be impossible if the Day of the Lord were to start at the beginning of Daniel's seventieth week (Isa. 2:12, 17)?

The fifth seal/event will be martyrdom during the Great Tribulation. Where did John see the souls of the martyrs (Rev. 6:9)?

Is this altar located in heaven or earth (Rev. 8:1-5)?

For what two reasons did they forfeit their lives (Rev. 6:9)?

How do these compare to the two reasons for John's suffering and banishment to the prison island of Patmos (Rev. 1:9)?

How do the reasons for their martyrdom compare to the reasons given in a parallel passage (Rev. 12:17)?

Personal Observations, Notes, or Quotes:

Whose wrath causes their suffering and martyrdom (Rev. 12:17; cf. Rev. 12:12; 13:4-7)?

Against whom do the martyrs wish their blood avenged (Rev. 6:10)?

Does their question indicate that God's wrath has already begun or are they asking for it to begin (Rev. 6:10)?

Do the martyrs believe God in His wrath is responsible for their bloodshed (Rev. 6:10)?

Who are these that "dwell on the earth" that Satan uses to carry out his attack (Rev. 13:8, 14)?

When later speaking of these martyrs, John further clarified the reasons for their persecution. What details does he add (Rev. 20:4)?

How does this compare to the stated program of the Antichrist (Rev. 13:15-17)?

Personal Observations, Notes, or Quotes:

II. *Cosmic Disturbance*

A. *In Relation to the Day of the Lord*

Cosmic disturbance is often connected to the Day of the Lord in the Bible. Summarize your findings for the following verses.

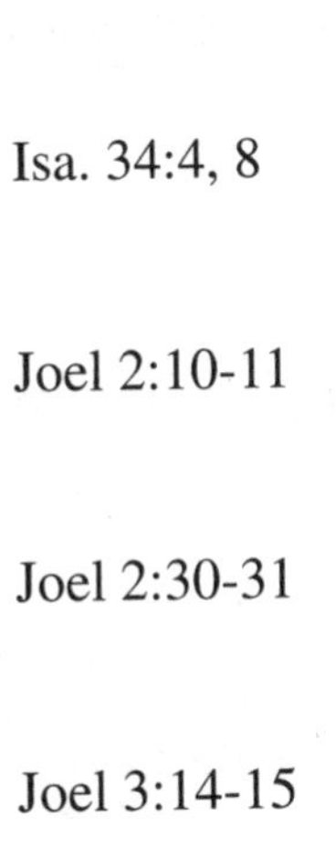

Isa. 13:9-10

Isa. 34:4, 8

Joel 2:10-11

Joel 2:30-31

Joel 3:14-15

Acts 2:19-20

When will this cosmic disturbance occur in relation to the Day of the Lord (Joel 2:31; Acts 2:20)?

Which seal in Revelation 6 describes this cosmic disturbance?

Personal Observations, Notes, or Quotes:

What can we conclude, therefore, about the timing of this seal in relation to the Day of the Lord?

If the Rapture occurs at the Day of the Lord and the Day of the Lord must be preceded by cosmic disturbance, what problem does this pose for those who hold to imminence?

B. *In Relation to the Great Tribulation*

What is the timing relationship of the cosmic disturbance to the Great Tribulation (Mt. 24:29; Mk. 13:24-25; Lk. 21:25-26)?

What can we conclude, therefore, about the timing of the Day of the Lord in relation to the Great Tribulation?

In the chart on the following page, label these important events or time periods: Antichrist signs a covenant, an abomination is placed in the Temple, the beginning of sorrows, the Great Tribulation, and the Day of the Lord. Refer back to your notes if you need to. After completing the chart, check yourself with the charts on pages 61 and 141 of *The Prewrath Rapture of the Church.*

Personal Observations, Notes, or Quotes:

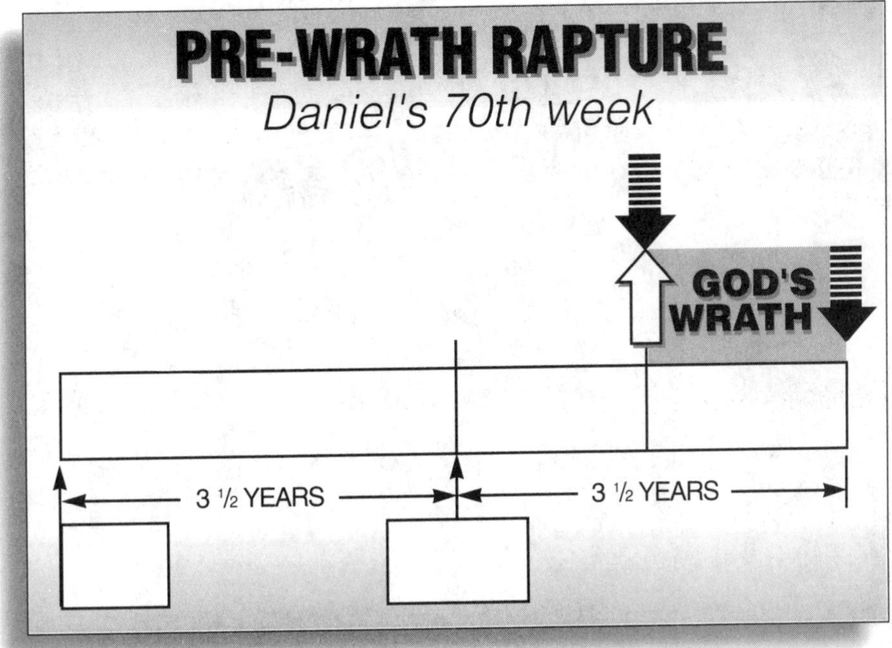

Personal Observations, Notes, or Quotes:

The PreWrath Rapture:

Every Piece Falls Right Into Place.

Elijah Must Appear First

Lesson Focus:
In this lesson you will study the prophet Elijah and his relationship to the second coming of Christ and the Day of the Lord.

Read Chapter 11 of *The Prewrath Rapture of the Church* before answering the following questions.

I. *Elijah's Relationship to the Two Witnesses*

Read Rev. 11:3-12 concerning the two future prophets in Israel.

How long will they witness (Rev. 11:3)?

What will be the condition of Jerusalem at that time (Rev. 11:2)?

From your earlier study, when does this happen to Jerusalem (Lk. 21:20)?

Personal Observations, Notes, or Quotes:

Therefore, when do the witnesses begin their ministry in relationship to Daniel's seventieth week?

What will they be able to do simply by the command of their mouth (Rev. 11:5)?

What other great prophet was given this power (1 Ki. 18:36-38; 2 Ki. 1:9-14)?

What other miracles will they be able to perform (Rev. 11:6)?

What prophet in the Old Testament was given the power to stop the rainfall (1 Ki. 17:1)?

How long will the two witnesses stop the rain (Rev. 11:6)?

How long was the rain stopped by the Hebrew prophet (Lk. 4:25; Jas. 5:17)?

What great prophet in the Old Testament was given the power to turn water into blood and perform other plagues (Ex. 7:20; 8:1-12:29)?

Personal Observations, Notes, or Quotes:

What were the circumstances surrounding the deaths of these great prophets which may suggest that they still have a future ministry as the two witnesses (Dt. 34:5-6; 2 Ki. 2:1-12; Jude 9)?

What two Old Testament prophets were given a preview of the glory of the Messiah in His kingdom at the transfiguration of Jesus (Mt. 17:1-9; Mk. 9:1-9; Lk. 9:28-36)?

What two Old Testament prophets are seen together in the prophetic passage of Malachi 4:4-6?

Under the Mosaic Law, matters of life and death required confirmation by at least two witnesses (Num. 35:30; Dt. 17:6; 19:15; Heb. 10:28). What are the life and death issues in the days of Antichrist that necessitate the two witnesses (Rev. 14:9-13)?

II. *Elijah's Relationship to the Day of the Lord*

Whom did the Lord promise to send (Mal. 4:5)?

When will He send him in relation to the Day of the Lord (Mal. 4:5)?

How does this pose a problem for imminence?

Personal Observations, Notes, or Quotes:

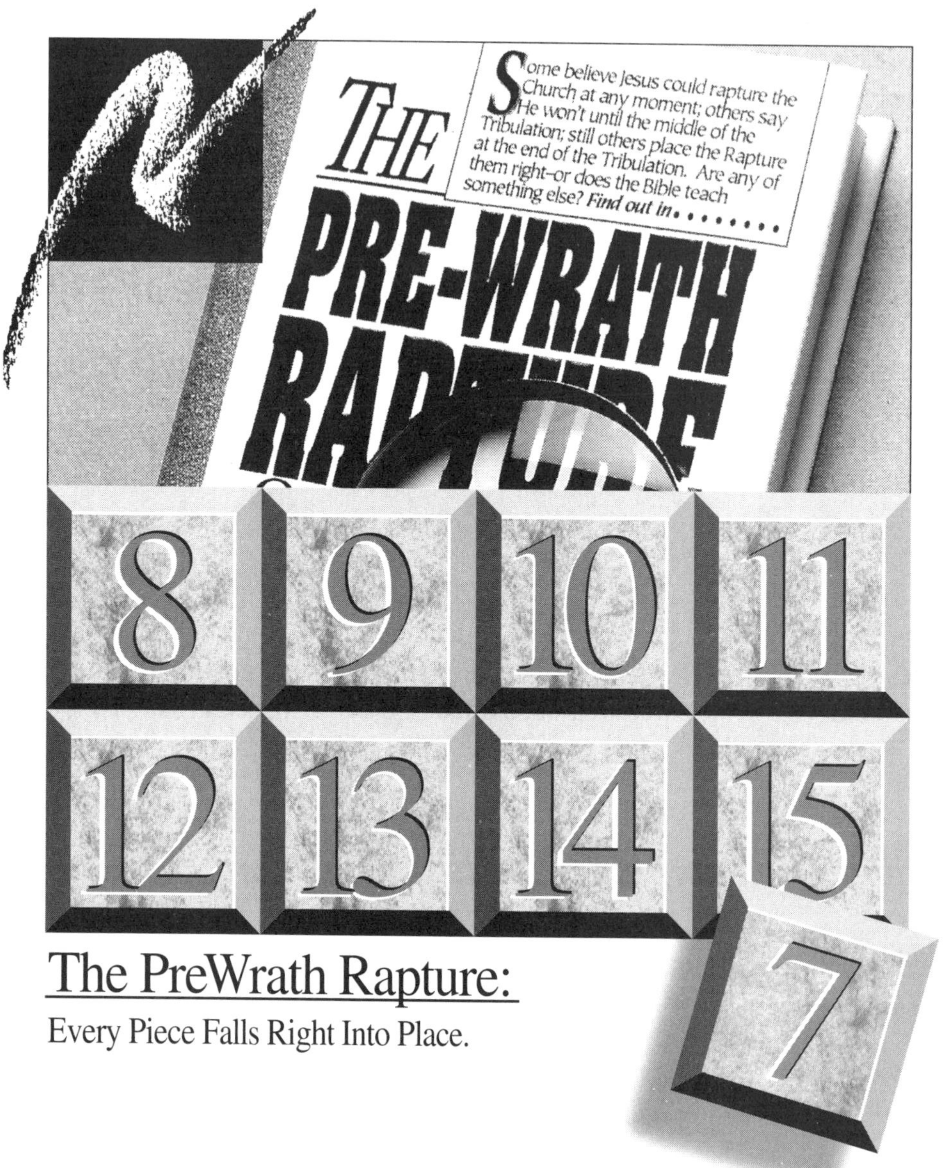

Some believe Jesus could rapture the Church at any moment; others say He won't until the middle of the Tribulation; still others place the Rapture at the end of the Tribulation. Are any of them right–or does the Bible teach something else? *Find out in........*

THE PRE-WRATH RAPTURE

The PreWrath Rapture:

Every Piece Falls Right Into Place.

The Day of His Wrath and the Last Trump

Lesson Focus:
In this lesson you will look at what the Book of Revelation says about God's wrath. You will also examine the historical use of the trumpet and its connection to the Rapture and the Day of the Lord.

Read Chapter 12 of *The Prewrath Rapture of the Church* before answering the following questions.

I. *The Day of God's Wrath*

What events occur when the sixth seal is opened (Rev. 6:12-14)?

Where will men flee (Rev. 6:15)?

What emotion will they display (Lk. 21:25-26)?

Personal Observations, Notes, or Quotes:

What parallels are found in Isaiah's description of the coming of the Day of the Lord (Isa. 2:12, 19-21; 13:6-10)?

The cosmic disturbance of the sixth seal will dramatically announce the coming of what day (Rev. 6:17)?

If the cosmic disturbance of the sixth seal announces the coming of that day, could that day have started at the first seal?

How does this agree with the Old Testament prophet (Joel 2:31)?

John said, in agreement with Isaiah (Isa. 2:17), Joel (Joel 2:11), and Nahum (Nah. 1:6), that no one will be able to stand (rebel successfully against the Lord) in the great day of His wrath. What did Malachi call the day of His wrath when no one will be able to stand (Mal. 3:2)?

John said the great day of His wrath "is come." What did Jesus mean by this exact word when He said, "the hour is come" regarding the timing of His betrayal and crucifixion (Mk. 14:41)? Had these events happened yet or were they just about to begin?

Personal Observations, Notes, or Quotes:

II. *The Occurrence of God's Wrath*

Look up the eight references to God's wrath in the Book of Revelation (Rev. 6:16-17; 11:18; 14:10; 15:2; 15:7; 16:1, 19).

At any time, is God's wrath seen before the seventh seal is ready to be opened which John calls "the great day of his wrath" (Rev. 6:16-17)?

Looking at the following chart, what conclusion concerning God's wrath can we draw about the trumpets and bowls since they come out of the seventh seal?

Personal Observations, Notes, or Quotes:

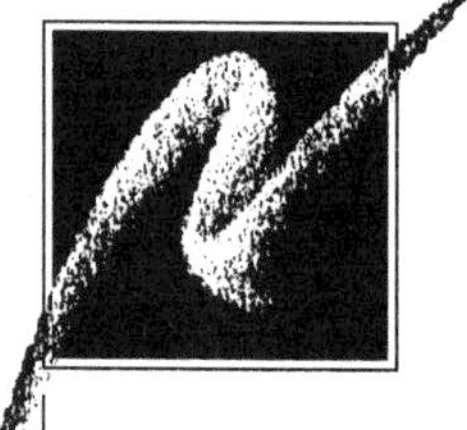

III. *The Last Trump*

Read Chapter 14 of *The Prewrath Rapture of the Church* before answering the following questions.

Why do you think Paul includes the Rapture (1 Cor. 15:51-53) in his discussion of the resurrection (1 Cor. 15:1-50)?

What three truths were always present in a biblical mystery? (p. 188)

What was the mystery that Paul spoke of in 1 Corinthians 15:51?

When will that event occur (1 Cor. 15:52)?

What were the two purposes of the Old Testament trumpet (Num. 10:2-3; Jer. 4:19)?

In a parallel passage to 1 Cor. 15:51-53, who does Paul say blows the last trump at the Rapture (1 Th. 4:16-17)?

Personal Observations, Notes, or Quotes:

Some have tried to associate the trumpet of the Rapture with the seventh trumpet in the Book of Revelation. Who blows the trumpets of Revelation including the seventh (Rev. 11:15)?

What future day is also connected to the blowing of the trumpet (Zeph. 1:14-16)?

Personal Observations, Notes, or Quotes:

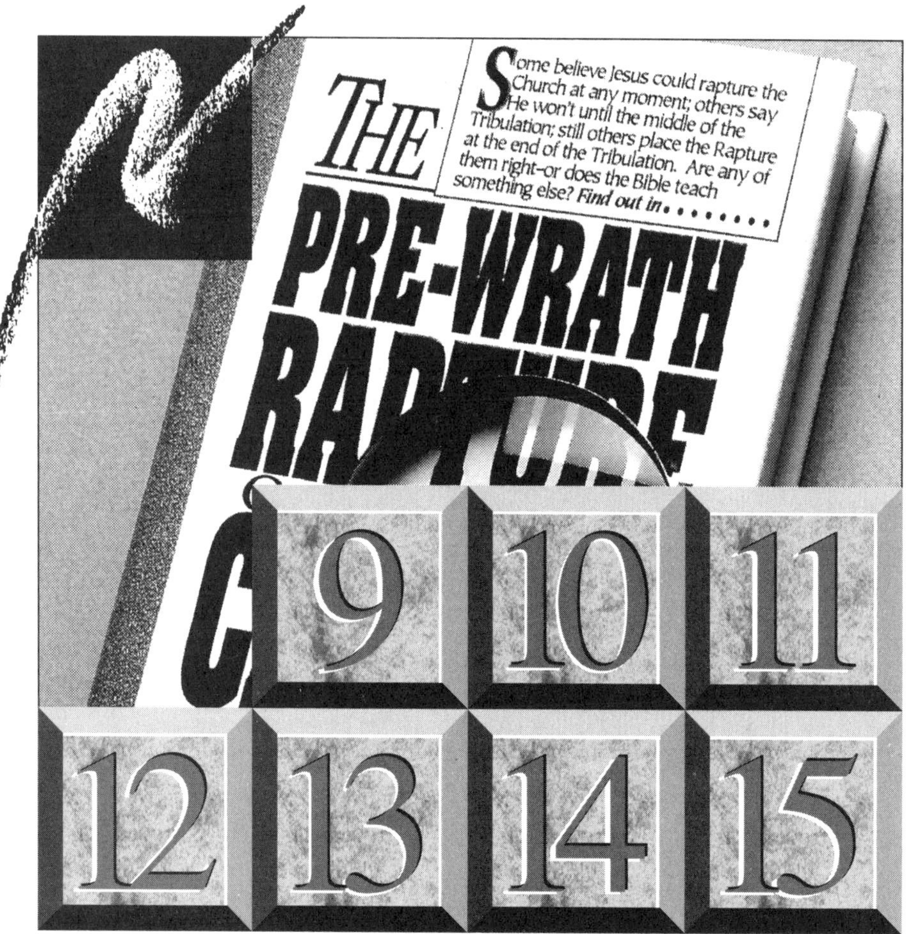

The PreWrath Rapture:

Every Piece Falls Right Into Place.

Examining

A Personal Study Guide

THE PREWRATH RAPTURE OF THE CHURCH

The 144,000 and a Great Multitude

Lesson Focus:

Following the opening of the first six seals and with the Day of the Lord about to begin, John described two groups of people — the 144,000 and a great multitude in Heaven that no man could number. In this lesson you will study these two groups of Revelation 7 to see whom they represent and why they appear at this precise time.

Read Chapter 13 of *The Prewrath Rapture of the Church* before answering the following questions.

I. *The 144,000*

Read Revelation 7:1-8 concerning the sealing of 144,000 of God's Jewish servants.

Does this occur before or after the opening of the sixth seal (Rev. 6:12)?

Does this occur before or after the opening of the seventh seal (Rev. 8:1)?

Personal Observations, Notes, or Quotes:

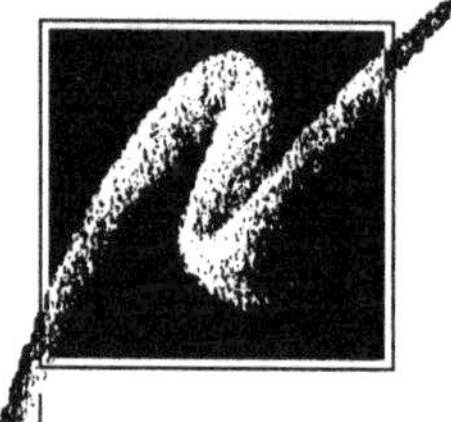

Whom did John see standing on the four corners of the earth (Rev. 7:1)?

What did they intend to do to the earth, the sea, and the trees until stopped by the angel from the east (Rev. 7:2-3)?

Were any of these things (the earth, the sea, or the trees) hurt during the first six seals (Rev. 6)?

Are any of these things (the earth, the sea, or the trees) hurt during the trumpet judgments which come out of the seventh seal (Rev. 8:6-11)?

Peter (2 Pet. 3:7, 10, 12), Paul (2 Th. 1:7-8), and the Old Testament prophets described the Lord's coming judgment as one of fire. Is fire found in any of the first six seals, and what might this indicate?

Fire is an integral element of the trumpets (Rev. 8:6-11). What might this indicate?

What did the angel from the east desire to do before the angels carried out the destructive judgment (Rev. 7:3)?

Personal Observations, Notes, or Quotes:

How many servants were sealed from each tribe (Rev. 7:4-8)?

What did sealing indicate in the ancient world? (pp. 143, 171)

In light of Revelation 6:17 and God's impending wrath, why do you think the 144,000 are sealed at this time instead of an earlier or later time?

II. *The Great Multitude*

Read Revelation 7:9-17 concerning the great multitude in Heaven.

Contrast the martyrs of the fifth seal (Rev. 6:9-11) and the great multitude in Heaven (Rev. 7:9-17).

How many are there?

Where are they located?

What are they saying?

Of what nationality or ethnic group is this great multitude (Rev. 7:9)?

Personal Observations, Notes, or Quotes:

John speaks of the great multitude as having bodies (i.e., standing, palms in hands, no more hunger or thirst). How does he describe the state of the fifth-seal martyrs as to whether they have bodies or not (Rev. 6:9)?

Does John say that the great multitude are martyrs?

If those of this great multitude have bodies, what great event for the Church must have occurred before this (1 Cor. 15:51-53; 1 Th. 4:16-17)?

What time period is cut short by the cosmic disturbance of the sixth seal (Mt. 24:21, 29)?

What did the great multitude in Heaven just come out of (Rev. 7:14)?

Does this great multitude appear in Heaven before or after the opening of the sixth seal (Rev. 6:12)?

Does this great multitude appear in Heaven before or after the opening of the seventh seal (Rev. 8:1)?

Personal Observations, Notes, or Quotes:

In light of Revelation 6:17 and God's impending wrath, why do you think this great multitude suddenly appears in Heaven at this time instead of an earlier or later time?

What promises do believers have concerning deliverance (salvation) from God's wrath (1 Th. 1:10; 5:9)?

For what action does this great multitude praise God (Rev. 7:10)?

In light of Revelation 6:17 and God's impending wrath, why do you think the great multitude in Heaven is praising God for salvation at this time (1 Th. 1:10; 5:9)?

Personal Observations, Notes, or Quotes:

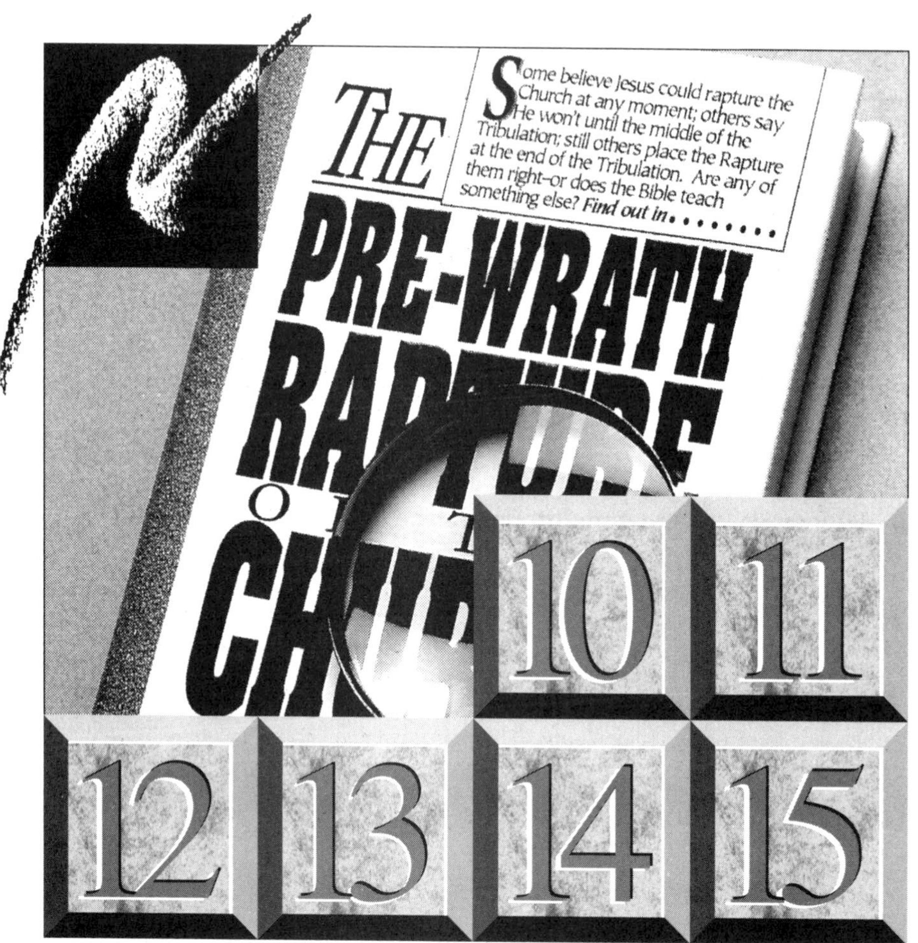

The PreWrath Rapture:

Every Piece Falls Right Into Place.

The Apostasy and the Man of Sin

Lesson Focus:

Paul's two letters to the Thessalonian church comprise the fullest treatment on Christ's second coming and the Rapture of the Church found anywhere in the Bible. In this lesson you will look at two precursors to the Day of the Lord cited by Paul to comfort the Thessalonian believers who thought they were already in the Day of the Lord.

Read Chapter 15 of *The Prewrath Rapture of the Church* before answering the following questions.

What false teaching troubled the church of Thessalonica (2 Th. 2:1-2)?

I. *The Apostasy*

What is the first event which Paul said will precede the Day of the Lord (2 Th. 2:3)?

The word for "falling away" (*apostasia,* Strong's #646) means a "defection, revolt, or apostasy" according to Vine's *Expository Dictionary of New Testament Words.* It signifies a *total abandonment.* How was the word (translated "forsake") used in its only other New Testament occurrence (Acts 21:21)?

Personal Observations, Notes, or Quotes:

How was the word used in the First Book of Maccabees and by Josephus to describe an earlier event in the history of Israel? (pp. 200-201)

What are some of the parallels between the Antichrist and his foreshadow, Antiochus Epiphanes? (pp. 202-205)

How will Israel abandon the Lord (apostatize) in the future and go after one who is not her husband (Isa. 28:15; Dan. 9:27)?

II. *The Man of Sin*

According to Paul, what is a second event which must occur before the Day of the Lord comes (2 Th. 2:3)?

How will the Antichrist be revealed (2 Th. 2:4; cf. Mt. 24:15)?

Personal Observations, Notes, or Quotes:

At what point will this occur in Daniel's seventieth week (Dan. 9:27; Rev. 13:5)?

If the Antichrist must be unveiled first by taking a seat in the Temple as God, must the Day of the Lord begin before or after the middle of Daniel's seventieth week?

If Paul taught that there are required prophetic events before the Rapture and the Day of the Lord, what can be said about the possibility of imminence according to the definition given by pretribulation rapturists?

Even though Paul taught that there would be precursors to the Day of the Lord, who did he teach was to be the believer's focus (1 Th. 1:10; Ti. 2:13)?

Personal Observations, Notes, or Quotes:

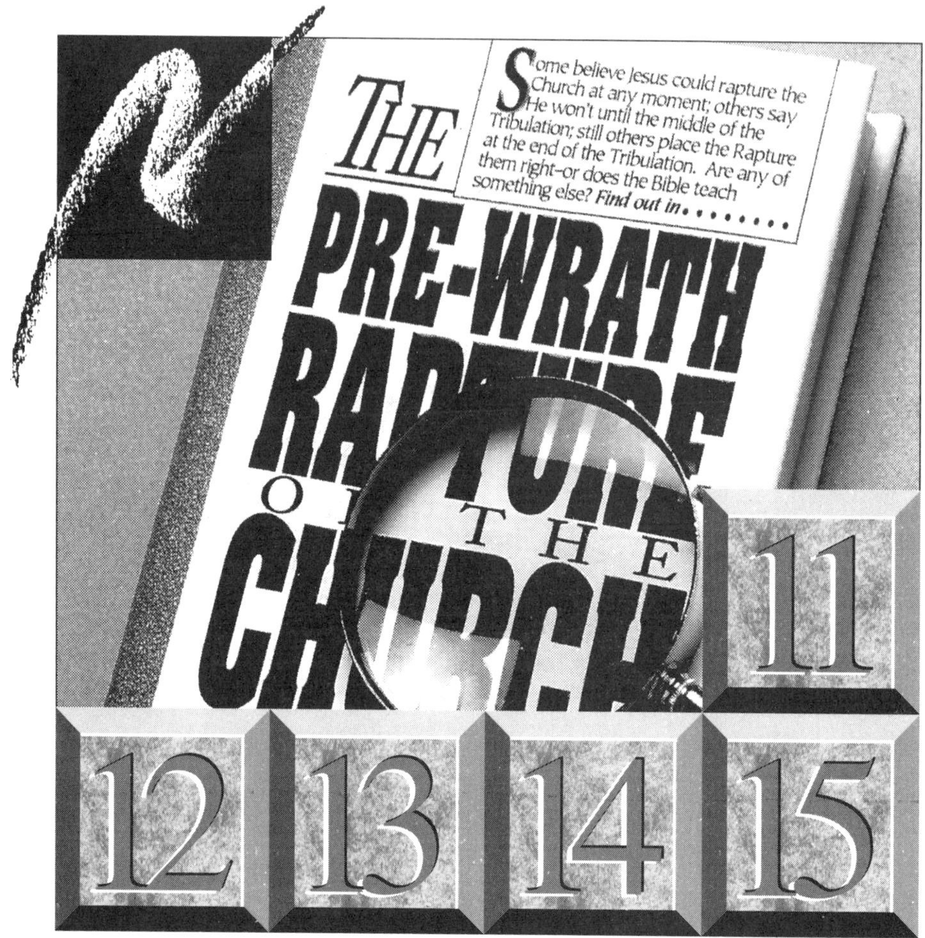

The PreWrath Rapture:

Every Piece Falls Right Into Place.

The Coming

Lesson Focus:

The disciples came to the Lord and asked, "What shall be the sign of thy coming, and of the end of the age?" (Mt. 24:3). In this lesson the first term of their question ("coming") will be examined to learn its definition, usage, and relationship to the timing of the Rapture.

Read pages 215-225 of Chapter 16 of *The Prewrath Rapture of the Church* before answering the following questions.

I. *The Definition of "Coming"*

State the meaning, and give one occurrence of the following Greek words as they are used in the New Testament to speak of Christ's second coming. (pp. 215-217)

Parousia (Strong's #3952):

Apokolupsis (Strong's #602):

Erchomai (Strong's #2064):

Epiphineia (Strong's #2015):

Personal Observations, Notes, or Quotes:

Which word did the disciples use when they asked, "What shall be the sign of thy coming" (Mt. 24:3)? (p. 215)

In what way does the word indicate more than just an arrival or coming? (p. 217)

II. *The Usage of "Coming"*

The word *parousia* occurs twenty-four times in the New Testament. In the King James Version of the Bible, the word *parousia* is translated "coming" twenty-two times, and two times it is translated "presence" (2 Cor. 10:10; Phil. 2:12). Eighteen times it is used prophetically — seventeen times of the coming of the Lord Jesus and once of the coming of Antichrist (2 Th. 2:9).

A. *Usage in General*

How is the word *parousia* translated in contrast to Paul's absence (Phil. 2:12)?

What did Paul pray for the Thessalonian church at the *parousia* or "coming" of our Lord Jesus Christ (1 Th. 3:13)?

How did Paul rephrase the same prayer just two chapters later when he again spoke of the *parousia* or "coming" of our Lord Jesus Christ (1 Th. 5:23)?

What was Peter's exhortation to those who look for the *parousia* of the Day of God (2 Pet. 3:12, 14)?

Personal Observations, Notes, or Quotes:

What does James command the Church to do until the *parousia* (coming) of the Lord (Jas. 5:7-8)?

What did John exhort believers to do so that they would not be "ashamed before him at his coming [*parousia*]" (1 Jn. 2:28)?

In light of these prayers, commands, and exhortations, will the Church be present until the *parousia* of Christ?

B. *Usage in Connection with the Rapture*

With what event does Paul equate the *parousia,* or coming of our Lord Jesus Christ (2 Th. 2:1)?

How does this compare to the events he had earlier told the Thessalonian church would occur at the *parousia* (1 Th. 4:15-17)?

What did Paul teach the Corinthian church regarding the timing of the resurrection of the righteous and the *parousia* of Christ (1 Cor. 15:21-23)?

Personal Observations, Notes, or Quotes:

Several verses later, Paul mentioned the resurrection again. When did he say it would occur (1 Cor. 15:52)?

C. *Usage in Connection with the Day of the Lord*

Peter prophesied that in the last days scoffers will arise and mock the "promise of his coming [*parousia*]" (2 Pet. 3:3-4). What will He do to the heavens and earth and ungodly men when He finally fulfills the promise of His *parousia* (2 Pet. 3:7)?

Why is the promise of His coming (*parousia*) not immediately fulfilled (2 Pet. 3:9)?

What day does Peter equate with His *parousia* (2 Pet. 3:10, 12)?

The Lord compared His *parousia* to the days of Noah when God's judgment suddenly fell upon the unsuspecting wicked and destroyed them all (Mt. 24:37, 39). How did Paul describe this same truth concerning the sudden coming of the Day of the Lord upon those in darkness (1 Th. 5:2-4)?

D. *Usage in Connection with the Glory*

The disciples asked Jesus concerning the sign of His *parousia* (Mt. 24:3). Where did Jesus say they would see that sign (Mt. 24:30)?

Personal Observations, Notes, or Quotes:

What will it cause the tribes of the earth to do (Mt. 24:30)?

What will they see concerning the sign of the Son of man that causes them to react in this way (Mt. 24:30; Mk. 13:26; Lk. 21:27)?

What does John say He will come with in a parallel passage (Rev. 1:7)?

What does Isaiah say will cause men to hide in the rocks at the Day of the Lord (Isa. 2:19, 21)?

To what bright light does Jesus compare His coming (Mt. 24:27; Lk. 17:24)?

What will the Lord do to the Antichrist through the brightness of Christ's *parousia* (2 Th. 2:8)?

How will the Lord be revealed from Heaven with mighty angels (2 Th. 1:7-8)?

In light of these verses, the sign of Christ's *parousia* or "presence" ties into an Old Testament concept. How did God manifest His unique presence to Moses (Ex. 3:2-6)?

Personal Observations, Notes, or Quotes:

What was the sign of His unique presence to Israel in the wilderness (Ex. 13:21)?

What was the sign of God's presence at Mt. Sinai (Ex. 24:17)?

How did the Lord manifest His presence at the dedication of the tabernacle (Ex. 33:9-10; 40:34-35)?

How did the Father manifest His presence at the transfiguration of the Messiah (Mt. 17:5)?

How does God manifest His presence in the heavenly temple (Rev. 15:8)?

On Target

This bright cloud of fire was called the Shekinah ("dwelling") glory of God by the Israelites for it indicated the dwelling of God's presence in their midst. The brilliant Shekinah glory cloud will also be the sign of Christ's parousia (coming and presence).

Even though Christ was not bodily present in Israel's wilderness experience, Paul taught that Christ was present and working in their midst (1 Cor. 10:1-4, 9). In light of the *Shekinah*, indicating God's presence, how was it possible for Paul to teach that Christ was in Israel's midst?

Personal Observations, Notes, or Quotes:

What promises do we have, as believers, concerning the future appearance of Christ's glory?

Col. 3:4

1 Pet. 4:13

Jude 24

In contrast to the *sign* of Christ's *parousia* which is manifested in the heavens, where will the *bodily* manifestation of Christ be seen throughout the day of His wrath (Rev. 7:9-10, 17)?

What will His followers be doing in Heaven during the day of His wrath (Rev. 7:9-10)?

III. *The Timing of His "Coming"*

What did Christ teach concerning the day and hour of His *parousia* (Mt. 24:36; Mk. 13:32)?

What did He teach would be possible to know concerning the *general time period* of His *parousia* (Mt. 24:32-34; Mk. 13:28-30; Lk. 21:28-32)?

Personal Observations, Notes, or Quotes:

How does this agree with Paul's teaching (1 Th. 5:4)?

What was Christ's exhortation to His followers in light of His *parousia* (Mt. 24:42-44; Mk. 13:32-37; Lk. 21:34)?

What was Paul's exhortation to the Thessalonian church (1 Th. 5:6)?

After what event/seal will the sign of Christ's *parousia* be seen (Mt. 24:29-30)?

Will this occur before or after the middle (Mt. 24:15) of Daniel's seventieth week?

If the *parousia* occurs at this time, what must be true of the timing of the Rapture and Day of the Lord based upon your study of their connection with the *parousia*?

Personal Observations, Notes, or Quotes:

Personal Observations, Notes, or Quotes:

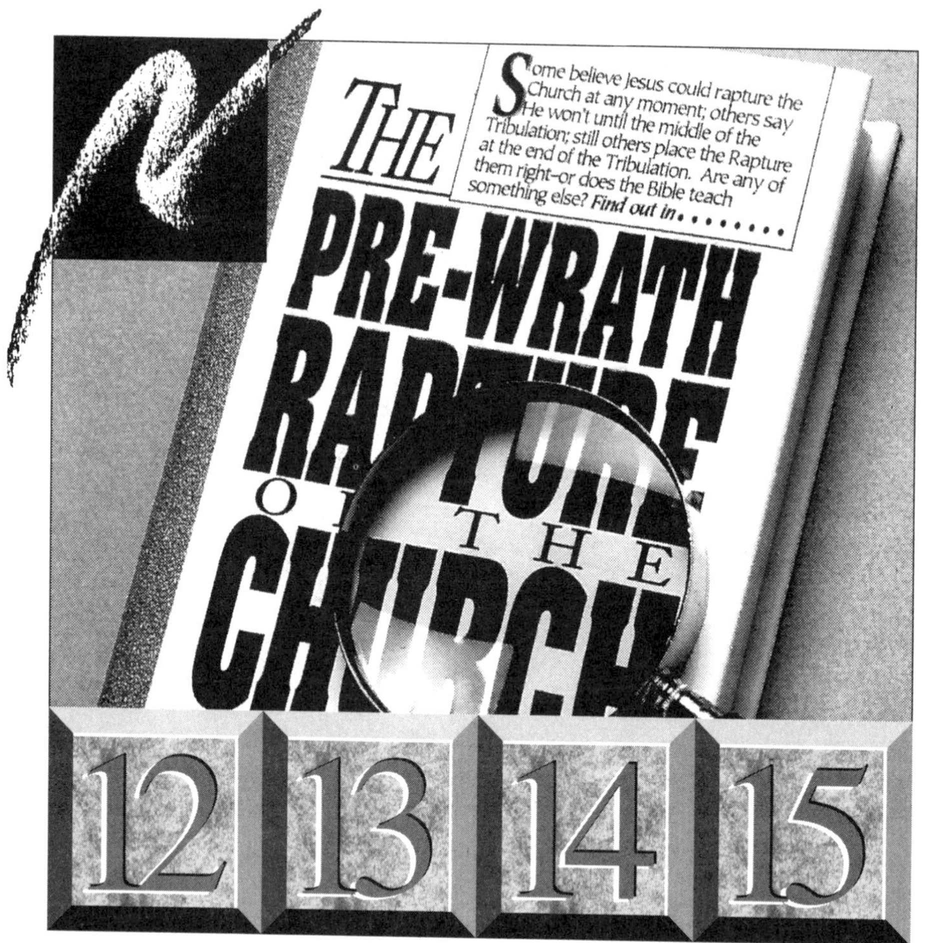

The PreWrath Rapture:

Every Piece Falls Right Into Place.

Examining

A Personal Study Guide

THE PREWRATH RAPTURE OF THE CHURCH

The End of the Age

Lesson Focus:

The disciples came to the Lord and asked, "What shall be the sign of thy coming, and of the end of the age?" (Mt. 24:3). In this lesson the second term of their question ("the end of the age") will be examined to learn its definition, usage, and relationship to the timing of the Rapture.

Read pages 225-230 of Chapter 16 of *The Prewrath Rapture of the Church* before answering the following questions.

I. *The Definition of "The End"*

What is the meaning of "world" (*aion,* Strong's #165) as the disciples used it in their Matthew 24:3 question? (p. 225)

Read the Lord's parable concerning the good seed and the tares, or weeds (Mt. 13:24-30) and His explanation (Mt. 13:36-43). With what term does Christ equate the harvest (Mt. 13:39)?

Personal Observations, Notes, or Quotes:

Who are the good seed that He said would be gathered into the barn at the end of the age (Mt. 13:38)?

Who are the tares that He said would be burned in the fire of His judgment at the end of the age (Mt. 13:38)?

John the Baptist said that Jesus would baptize with the Holy Spirit (His first coming) and with fire (His second coming). What did he say that Jesus will do with the wheat at the harvest (Mt. 3:12)?

To what event do you think this gathering referred (1 Th. 4:17; 2 Th. 2:1)?

What will Jesus do with the chaff (Mt. 3:12)?

II. *The Usage of "The End"*

The disciples asked Jesus, "What shall be the sign of thy coming (*parousia*) and of the end of the world?" (Mt. 24:3). They spoke of a sign in the singular, reflecting their belief that one sign would indicate both events — His *parousia* and the end of the age. They understood that at His *parousia* He would harvest the wheat into the barn. Look up 1 Corinthians 15:23-24 and 1 Thessalonians 3:13 and notice how Paul also equated the *parousia* with the end.

Personal Observations, Notes, or Quotes:

With what day did Paul connect the end (1 Cor. 1:8; 2 Cor. 1:13-14)?

With what revelation/coming (*apokalupsis,* Strong's #602) do Paul and Peter equate the end (1 Cor. 1:7-8; 1 Pet. 1:13)?

As Jesus commissioned and commanded the Church to evangelize the world, He promised to be with them "always" until what time (Mt. 28:20)?

III. *The Time of "The End"*

Returning to the disciples' question, let us examine the Lord's reply to their inquiry about the end of the age.

After the description of what two events/seals did Jesus say that the end would not yet have occurred (Mt. 24:4-6; Mk. 13:5-7; Lk. 21:8-9)?

Was He describing events inside or outside Daniel's seventieth week at this point?

What events/seals did He go on to describe (Mt. 24:7-10; Mk. 13:8-12; Lk. 21:11-19)?

Personal Observations, Notes, or Quotes:

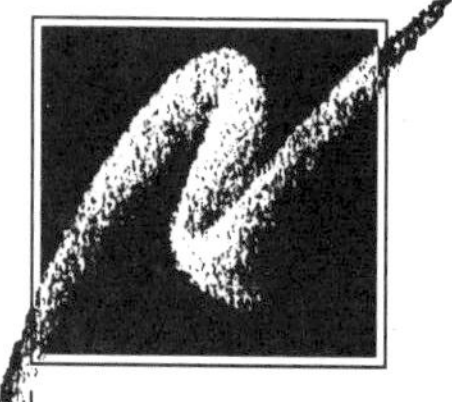

When the Lord taught that the end would come, was the context of His discussion inside or outside Daniel's seventieth week (Mt. 24:13-14)?

The Lord taught that the end would come after the fifth seal. What is the fifth seal?

Is this at the beginning or after the middle of Daniel's seventieth week?

Therefore, must the end of the age occur before or after the middle of Daniel's seventieth week?

IV. *Those Who Endure to "The End"*

In connection with the discussion of that event, what did Jesus teach concerning the end and those to be delivered (Mt. 24:13; Mk. 13:13)?

The word "endure" (*hupomeno,* Strong's #5278) means to suffer trials patiently and to persevere. In context, during what seal/event are believers persevering (Mt. 24:9-12; Mk. 13:9-13)?

Personal Observations, Notes, or Quotes:

In a connected thought, the Greek word *perileipo* ("remain," Strong's #4035) is only used twice in the New Testament. Both times it occurs in Paul's discussion of the Rapture (1 Th. 4:15, 17). The normal Greek word for "remain" is *meno,* (Strong's #3306) but *perileipo* conveys the idea of "survive."

Paul taught that the dead in Christ would be resurrected first. Who, then, would be raptured (1 Th. 4:15-17)?

Paul spoke of Church believers who "remain" or "survive." In light of Matthew 24:13, what is it that they survive to be raptured?

In this lesson you have seen that the end is connected to and consistent with the timing of the *parousia* of Christ and the Day of the Lord. According to Scripture, will these events occur before or after the middle of Daniel's seventieth week?

If the Church is commanded to evangelize until the end of the age (Mt. 28:18-20), what does this tell you as to whether the Church will go into Daniel's seventieth week or not?

Personal Observations, Notes, or Quotes:

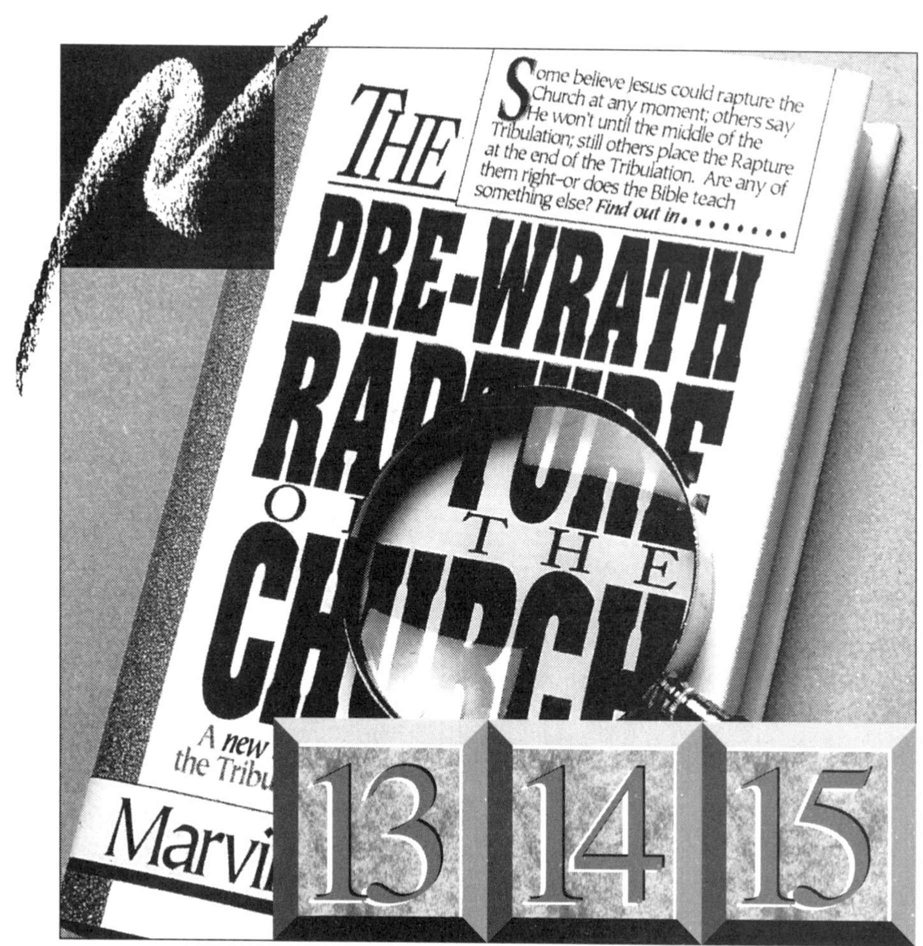

The PreWrath Rapture:

Every Piece Falls Right Into Place.

A Personal Study Guide

Examining

THE PREWRATH RAPTURE OF THE CHURCH

Kept From the Hour

Lesson Focus:
The resurrected Lord's message to the church of Philadelphia was one of comfort. He promised, "Because thou has kept the word of my patience, I also will keep thee from the hour of temptation" (Rev. 3:10). This verse, for many theologians, has become the watershed in the debate over the timing of the Rapture. In this lesson you will look at this controversial verse and its relationship to the Rapture.

Read Chapter 17 of *The Prewrath Rapture of the Church* before answering the following questions.

I. *Kept the Word of My Patience*

The word "patience" (*hupomone,* Strong's #5281) occurs twenty-eight times in the New Testament. What is the basic meaning of the word "patience"? (p. 235)

The church of Philadelphia was commended for keeping the word of His patience (Rev. 3:10). What is "the patience of the saints" as they patiently persevere and endure (Rev. 14:12)?

Personal Observations, Notes, or Quotes:

In Lesson 5 you saw that keeping the words (or commandments) of God and the testimony (or faith) of Jesus were connected elsewhere in the Book of Revelation. John suffered tribulation as a result of keeping these (Rev. 1:9). The martyrs of the fifth seal will be slain for these two things (Rev. 6:9; 20:4). The saints during the Great Tribulation will patiently endure persecution because of these two (Rev. 12:17; 14:12). Later, in describing John's brethren as the bride of Christ called to the marriage supper of the Lamb, what was it that they also steadfastly held (Rev. 19:9-10)?

In His message to the Philadelphia church, what did the Lord connect with keeping His word (Rev. 3:8)?

The Philadelphia church did not deny the name of Jesus. With whom does John identify those who deny the Father and the Son (1 Jn. 2:22)?

What did the Lord promise to those who, at His coming, are ashamed of (deny) these two important things mentioned in the Book of Revelation — Christ and His commandments (Lk. 9:26)?

How does this parallel Christ's warnings and promises in another passage (Mt. 10:32-33)?

What danger did Christ teach would be present that might cause men to deny Him (Mt. 10:28)?

Personal Observations, Notes, or Quotes:

How is this like the adversity patiently endured by the saints during the Great Tribulation (Lk. 21:12-19; Rev. 13:10)?

According to Jesus, why will the world hate believers during the Great Tribulation (Mt. 24:9; Mk. 13:13; Lk. 21:17)?

II. *Will Keep Thee*

The Lord promised to keep them (*tereo,* Strong's #5083), *to guard or protect in a sphere of danger,* because they had kept the word of His patience (Rev. 3:10).

III. *The Test*

The word "temptation" (*peirasmos,* Strong's #3986) occurs twenty-one times in the New Testament. What is the explicit meaning of this word? (p. 238)

What is the test that the Antichrist will impose upon the whole world during the Great Tribulation (Rev. 13:15-17)?

What will happen to those who identify with the Antichrist through this test (Rev. 14:9-11)?

Personal Observations, Notes, or Quotes:

Where are those who refuse to identify with the Antichrist later seen (Rev. 15:1-2)?

What promise do the godly have from the Lord concerning temptation (*peirasmos*) (2 Pet. 2:9)?

Will He deliver the godly "before" or "out of" testing (2 Pet. 2:9)?

What warning do the unjust have (2 Pet. 2:9)?

IV. *From the Hour*

The Greek preposition *ek*, meaning "out of, from within," is translated "from" in the King James Version. It is the focal point of the Rapture debate surrounding Revelation 3:10. Pretribulation rapturists generally understand *ek* to mean "removal" from the temptation. Posttribulation rapturists interpret *ek* to mean "protection from" the temptation. Returning to its basic meaning, "out from within," *ek* simply shows the emergence of the faithful Church. It indicates that the Church is removed, delivered, or raptured "out from within" the Great Tribulation or the hour of testing (*peirasmos,* Strong's #3986) after being protected in it.

Four chapters after the message to the church of Philadelphia, John saw a great multitude in Heaven. Where had this great multitude come *ek,* or "out from within" (Rev. 7:14)?

Personal Observations, Notes, or Quotes:

If the Church comes "out from within" the hour of testing
(the Great Tribulation), must the Church be raptured before or after the middle of
Daniel's seventieth week when the Great Tribulation begins?

Personal Observations, Notes, or Quotes:

The PreWrath Rapture:

Every Piece Falls Right Into Place.

A Personal Study Guide

Examining

THE PREWRATH RAPTURE OF THE CHURCH

Are Pretribulation Rapture Arguments Really Unanswerable? Part 1

Lesson Focus:

In a discussion of the timing of the Rapture, objections are sometimes raised against the prewrath Rapture. What are these objections? Do they have any biblical basis? Do they really pose a problem for a prewrath Rapture view? In this lesson you will look at some of these most-often-cited objections in light of God's Word.

Read Chapter 18 of *The Prewrath Rapture of the Church* before answering the following questions.

I. *The Blessed Hope*

OBJECTION

Pretribulation rapturists sometimes assert that the Rapture is no longer the "blessed hope" if the Church is to first suffer persecution under the wrath of Antichrist.

ANALYSIS

From your earlier studies, are believers ever promised exemption from tribulation?

Personal Observations, Notes, or Quotes:

13

From what does God promise to deliver believers (1 Th. 1:10; 5:9)?

Paul experienced great tribulation in his life (Acts 20:23-24; 2 Cor. 11:23-27; Col. 1:24). How did this affect Paul's confidence in the blessed hope (Ti. 2:13)?

Peter also experienced great affliction without diminishing his hope of future rapture and home in Heaven (1 Pet. 1:4-7). What did he call this hope which we look forward to (1 Pet. 1:3)?

In light of the examples of Paul and Peter (who were part of the Church), does the possibility of tribulation diminish the reality or nature of the "blessed hope"?

II. *The Twenty-Four Elders*

OBJECTION

Many pretribulationists argue that the twenty-four elders of Revelation 4 represent the Church. Therefore, the Church cannot be raptured prewrath in Revelation 7 (just before the seventh seal) because the Church would already be in Heaven (Rev. 4) as represented by the twenty-four elders.

ANALYSIS

A. *The Twenty-Four Elders and the Church*

Personal Observations, Notes, or Quotes:

Are the twenty-four elders anywhere identified as representatives of the Church in Revelation 4?

Read Revelation 4 and 5. Aside from the debated twenty-four elders, did John see the Church in Heaven?

If he did not see the Church in Heaven, where does the Church have to be?

B. *The Twenty-Four Elders and Their Crowns*

The church of Smyrna was promised a victor's crown (*stephanos*) for their faithfulness (Rev. 2:10). Some argue that since the twenty-four elders are wearing crowns (*stephanos*), this proves that they are part of the glorified Church in Heaven. However, who else is pictured as wearing a crown (*stephanos*) in the Book of Revelation (Rev. 6:1-2)?

Does this prove that he is part of the Church?

C. *The Twenty-Four Elders and Their Number*

What other group in Scripture was comprised of twenty-four representatives and may explain the twenty-four elders (1 Chr. 24:1-19)?

Personal Observations, Notes, or Quotes:

III. *The Restrainer*

OBJECTION

Paul wrote to the Thessalonians concerning events that would occur before the Day of the Lord: "For the mystery of iniquity doth already work; only he who now hindereth will continue to hinder until he be taken out of the way. And then shall that wicked one be revealed, whom the Lord shall consume with the spirit of his mouth, and shall destroy with the brightness of his coming" (2 Th. 2:7-8). Pretribulation rapturists argue that this restrainer is the Holy Spirit, and He ceases to hinder when He is taken out of the world with the raptured Church, allowing the Antichrist to come on the scene.

ANALYSIS

A. *The Holy Spirit*

What will happen when the restrainer ceases to hinder (2 Th. 2:8)?

In the immediate context, Paul taught that the Antichrist will be revealed by sitting in the Temple (2 Th. 2:3-4). According to your earlier study, does this unveiling of the Antichrist in the Temple occur at the beginning or midpoint of Daniel's seventieth week?

Therefore, in context, when must the restrainer stop hindering?

How does this pose a problem for pretribulation rapturists who believe the Holy Spirit is the restrainer?

Personal Observations, Notes, or Quotes:

From your earlier studies, when do the events of Mark 13:9-23 (see especially verse 14) take place? Before or during Daniel's seventieth week?

Who do you find giving guidance to believers during the Great Tribulation (Mk. 13:11)?

How does this pose a problem for pretribulation rapturists who believe the Holy Spirit is the restrainer?

From your knowledge, is the Holy Spirit ever called the restrainer in Scripture?

B. *Michael*

1. *In Daniel*

What does the word "hinder" mean? (p. 257)

Who is the prince and guardian of Israel (Dan. 10:21)?

What is Michael's rank among angelic forces (Dan. 10:13)?

Personal Observations, Notes, or Quotes:

What does Michael's name mean? (p. 257)

Who, as God's enemy, and in opposition to Michael's name, desires to be "like the Most High" (Isa. 14:14)?

Who is Michael seen contending with over the body of Moses (Jude 9)?

On Target

The Hebrew word ***amad*** *(Strong's #5975) means "to arise or cease," depending upon the previous state of a person. If one is sitting and performs the action of* ***amad****, it means "to arise." If one is walking and performs the action of* ***amad****, it means "to cease." It can also mean "withstand or stand fast."*

What type of activity (peace/warfare) was Michael engaged in with the prince of Persia, another angelic being (Dan. 10:13, 20)?

Is this activity normally done while sitting down?

How did Daniel describe Michael's activity in Daniel 10:21?

Personal Observations, Notes, or Quotes:

The word "holdeth" (*chazaq,* Strong's #2388) means "to fasten upon, to seize, be strong, obstinate, to bind, *restrain.*" How does this compare to the meaning of "hinder"? (p. 257)

So, in this case, does the Bible say that Michael is acting as a restrainer?

If he is already "standing fast" for Daniel's people and then performs the action of *amad*, does he cease or arise?

What type of time will there be for Israel as a result of Michael performing this action (Dan. 12:1)?

Does this sound like he is fighting for Israel or has ceased to "stand fast" for Israel?

Where will the Antichrist place his headquarters at this time (Dan. 11:45)?

When will the Antichrist reveal himself in the Temple (Dan. 9:27; Rev. 11:2; 12:6, 14; 13:5)?

How does this compare to what you have already learned concerning when the Great Tribulation begins in Daniel's seventieth week?

Personal Observations, Notes, or Quotes:

So when in Daniel's seventieth week will Michael perform the action of *amad* or, in other words, cease withstanding the enemies of Daniel's people?

From what you studied earlier, *when* will the restrainer cease hindering so that the Antichrist can be revealed in the Temple?

Does this coincide with the timing of Michael's action?

2. *In Revelation*

In Revelation 12:1-5, who is the woman (nation) that gives birth to the man child who is to rule all nations (Rev. 12:5)?

John saw war in Heaven. Who (Michael or the Holy Spirit) is seen warring against Satan (Rev. 12:7)?

What was the outcome (Rev. 12:8-10)?

What are the feelings of the devil as he comes down (Rev. 12:12)?

Personal Observations, Notes, or Quotes:

What does he know that causes this emotion (Rev. 12:12)?

Whom does he go after to persecute (Rev. 12:13)?

Where does she find refuge during this time of trouble (Rev. 12:6, 14)?

How long does she find refuge there during this time of her trouble (Rev. 12:6, 14)?

As you have already seen, when did Daniel say that Michael would "cease" (*amad*) and the most troublesome time of Israel's history would result (Dan. 12:1)?

As Michael shifts his activities to Heaven instead of upon Israel, what happens to Israel (Rev. 12:13)?

What does this allow Satan to do to Antichrist (Rev. 13:4)?

When will Satan empower the Antichrist (Rev. 13:5)?

Does this fit the timing of when the restrainer ceases to hinder which, in turn, allows the Antichrist to be revealed in the Temple (2 Th. 2:7-8)?

Personal Observations, Notes, or Quotes:

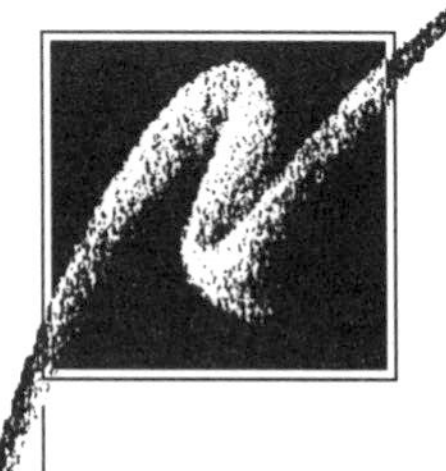

The only other *future* reference to Michael finds him participating in activity in the heavens and not actively fighting for Israel on earth. In what great future event does he take part (1 Th. 4:16-17)?

In another *future* passage, an angel (which may or may not be Michael) is seen in connection with Satan's restraint during the 1,000-year kingdom. What does this angel do to Satan (Rev. 20:1-3)?

Based on your study of the Bible, is it possible for another angelic being, empowered by the sovereign God, to restrain Satan?

IV. *Dispensationalism*

OBJECTION

Pretribulation rapturists argue that a consistent dispensational approach to Scripture — one that keeps God's workings with the nation of Israel and with the Church distinct — leads unerringly to pretribulational rapturism. They assert that since the Church was not in Daniel's first sixty-nine weeks, it cannot be in the seventieth week.

ANALYSIS

In regard to the starting point of the Church, why was it historically impossible for the Church to be in the first sixty-nine weeks (which ended with Calvary)? (p. 263)

Personal Observations, Notes, or Quotes:

From a strictly historical point of view, is it possible for the Church to be in Daniel's seventieth week?

From your earlier study, when the Lord begins to work with the 144,000 from national Israel (12,000 from each tribe) in Revelation 7:1-8, does this occur at the beginning of Daniel's seventieth week or after the midpoint?

Therefore, at what point of time would the Church need to be raptured to keep it distinct from God's program with national Israel?

What group does John see in Heaven at that moment (Rev. 7:9)?

Personal Observations, Notes, or Quotes:

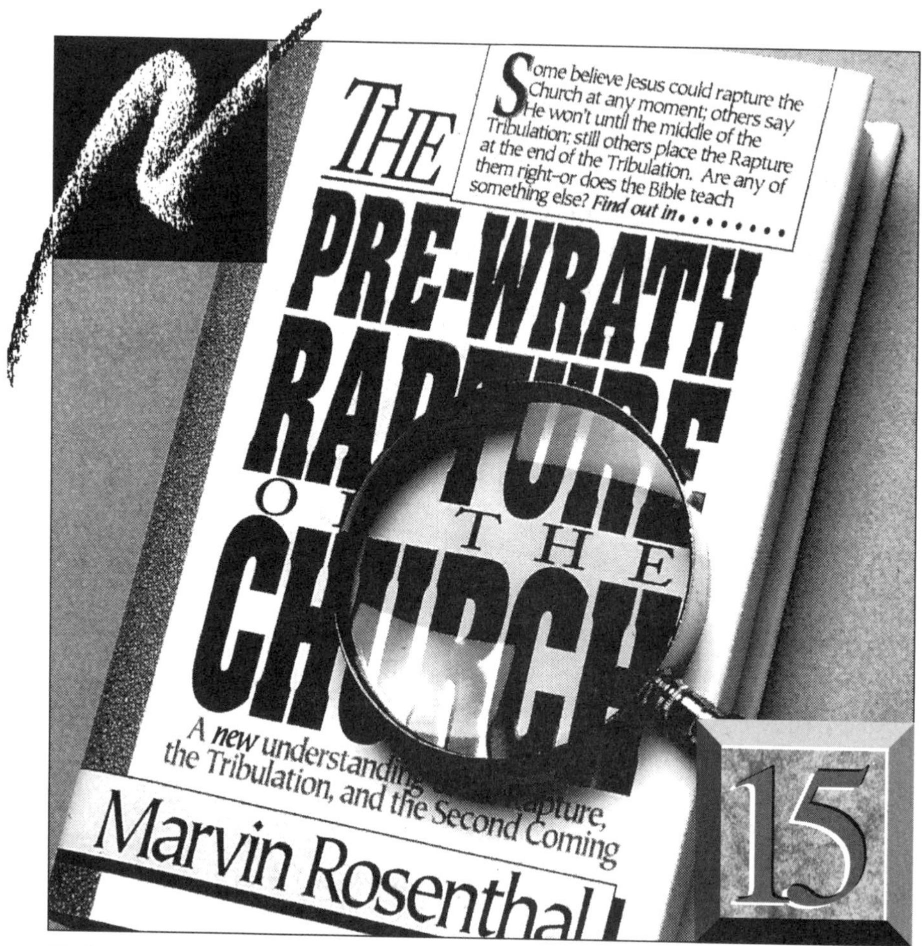

The PreWrath Rapture:

Every Piece Falls Right Into Place.

Are Pretribulation Rapture Arguments Really Unanswerable? Part 2

Lesson Focus:
In this lesson you will continue your study of objections which are sometimes raised against the prewrath Rapture.

I. *A Postulated Gap*

OBJECTION

Some pretribulation rapturists have realized the overwhelming biblical evidence for the Day of the Lord beginning at the seventh seal. Yet, instead of embracing a prewrath Rapture position, they have postulated a gap of time between the Rapture and the Day of the Lord. This allows them to maintain their pretribulation rapturism and accept the starting point of the Day of the Lord at the seventh seal. Does the Bible allow for such a gap, or does the Rapture and the beginning of the Day of the Lord occur simultaneously?

ANALYSIS

A. *Watching*

Personal Observations, Notes, or Quotes:

1. *The Event*

Our Lord taught that "heaven and earth shall pass away" (Lk. 21:33). What did Peter call the day when the heavens and earth (elements) will pass away (2 Pet. 3:10, 12)?

How did the Lord describe the coming of that day (Lk. 21:34-35)?

How did Peter say it would come (2 Pet. 3:10)?

How did Paul say it would come (1 Th. 5:2)?

2. *The Command*

What activity did the Lord command so that His followers would be warned of the coming of that day (Lk. 21:36)?

According to Peter, what should believers be doing until that day (2 Pet. 3:12)?

What did Paul exhort believers to do so that that day would not overtake them as a thief (1 Th. 5:4, 6)?

Personal Observations, Notes, or Quotes:

Could believers be commanded to watch for that day if they will never see it but be raptured years earlier?

B. *Revealed From Heaven*

When Christ is "revealed from Heaven," what will He do to those who do not know Him (2 Th. 1:7-9)?

Will the Church saints still be present on earth in the day that He is "revealed from heaven" (2 Th. 1:10)?

Is it possible to have a gap here between the time He raptures them and the time He begins His fiery vengeance in the Day of the Lord?

C. *The Disciples' Question*

What did the disciples ask for that would indicate the coming of the Lord and the end of the age (Mt. 24:3)?

Did they ask for a singular or plural indicator?

Personal Observations, Notes, or Quotes:

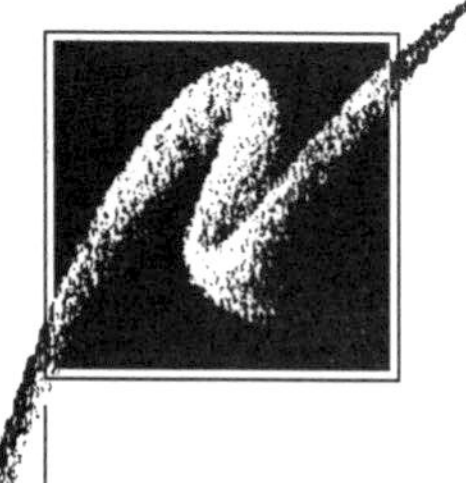

Based upon this, do you think the disciples viewed these two events (the coming and the end of the age in which He delivers the righteous and judges the wicked) as events separated by time or as simultaneous events?

D. *Until the Day*

How long will God perform the good work that He has begun in us (Phil. 1:6)?

Until when does Paul wish the Philippian believers to be "sincere and without offense" (Phil. 1:10)?

Paul exhorted these believers to be *blameless* so that he could rejoice in what day (Phil. 2:15-16)?

In what condition did Peter exhort his readers to be found when the Day of God comes (2 Pet. 3:12, 14)?

What action did Paul exhort the Corinthian church to do until the coming of the Lord (1 Cor. 1:7)?

Personal Observations, Notes, or Quotes:

What condition did he desire them to be found in at the Day of our Lord Jesus Christ (1 Cor. 1:8)?

In every instance of Scripture God will perform His good work, and believers are to continue living holy lives *until* the Day of the Lord. There is no gap of time allowed by Scripture.

E. *The Lord's Comparison*

1. *Noah*

Jesus compared His coming with the days of Noah. The wicked carried on the normal activities of life, totally unaware that God was about to intervene in human affairs (Mt. 24:37-39; Lk. 17:26-27). Until what day were they unprepared (Lk. 17:27)?

How long before the Flood did God command Noah to begin gathering the animals into the ark (Gen. 7:1-4)?

What occurred seven days later on the six hundredth year, second month, and seventeenth day of Noah's life (Gen. 7:11-12)?

What did Noah and his family do on that "very same" day that the Flood began (Gen. 7:13)?

Personal Observations, Notes, or Quotes:

Was there a gap of time between Noah entering the ark and the beginning of the Flood?

In light of this, what do you think the Lord's point was regarding His coming to deliver the righteous and destroy the wicked (Lk. 17:26-27)?

What happened to those left behind (not taken into the ark) in the day of Noah (Gen. 7:23)?

In light of this, what do you think the Lord was teaching about those who are left behind at His coming (Mt. 24:40-41; Lk. 17:34-36)?

2. *Lot*

Jesus went on to compare His coming with the day of Lot. On which day did the Lord deliver Lot in relation to the day he rained fire and brimstone from Heaven to destroy Sodom (Lk. 17:29)?

How is this like the day of His coming when He is revealed from Heaven (Lk. 17:30)?

Personal Observations, Notes, or Quotes:

In light of Luke 17:29-30, is it possible to have a gap of time between the Lord's deliverance (Rapture) and judgment (Day of the Lord)?

What happened to the inhabitants of the cities who remained behind in the day of Lot? Were they delivered or destroyed (Gen. 19:17, 25)?

In light of this, what was the Lord's message concerning those who remain behind at His coming (Lk. 17:34-36)?

II. *Taken to Be With the Lord*

OBJECTION

Pretribulation rapturists often refer to John 14:1-3 as a proof that the Church will be raptured to spend the entire seven years of Daniel's seventieth week in Heaven. They draw an analogy to the ancient Jewish marriage custom where the bridegroom, after preparing a dwelling place, would come and take his bride-to-be to his father's house for the wedding. After the wedding ceremony, the bride would be hidden away in the bridal chamber, sometimes for seven days (although it varied) while the wedding feast took place. They say these seven days represent the seven years of Daniel's seventieth week and, therefore, the Church must be in Heaven for seven years.

ANALYSIS

Did Jesus make a connection to the Jewish wedding in John 14:1-3 or speak about seven days or equate them to seven years in Heaven with Him?

Personal Observations, Notes, or Quotes:

After the Lord has prepared a place for us in His Father's house, He will come again. What will He do for us then (Jn. 14:3)?

Nine times Jesus used the Greek word *paralambano* meaning "take or receive into one's presence." Three times He used it in a nonprophetic context (Mt. 12:45; 18:16; Lk. 11:26). In John 14:3, an uncontested second coming verse, He used *paralambano* to refer to the Rapture when He said He would receive us unto Himself.

The other five times that Jesus used this word *paralambano*, He did so in the context of His second coming. If He was consistent with His usage in John 14:3, what did He mean when He said some would be taken or received (*paralambano*) at His second coming (Mt. 24:40-41; Lk. 17:34-36)?

In the other passages, He drew a comparison to Noah (Mt. 24:37-39; Lk. 17:26-27). What happened (deliverance/destruction) to those received into Noah's ark?

What happened to those who were not received into Noah's ark (Gen. 7:23)?

Personal Observations, Notes, or Quotes:

Personal Observations, Notes, or Quotes:

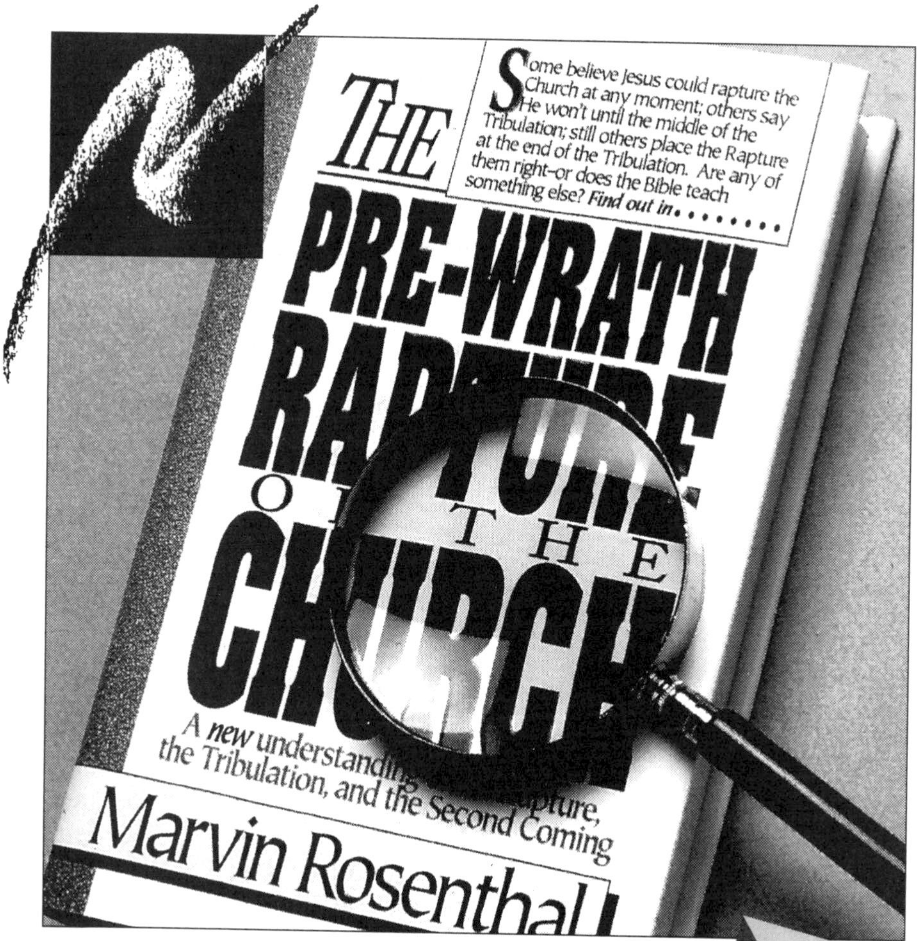

The PreWrath Rapture:

Every Piece Falls Right Into Place.

15

Examining

A Personal Study Guide

THE PREWRATH RAPTURE OF THE CHURCH

15

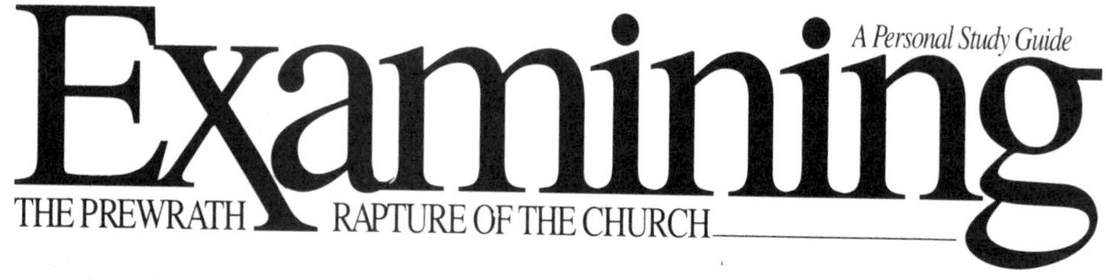

Final Matters

Lesson Focus:
In this lesson you will take a closer look at the concept of *imminence* in light of God's Word. You will also examine the teachings of the early church fathers to determine their view concerning the timing of the Rapture. Finally, you will look at the practical implications related to the timing of Christ's return and their absolute relevance to godly living on a daily basis.

I. *Imminence*

Read the article in Appendix A of this study guide by Marv Rosenthal entitled, *Imminence*, before answering the following questions.

What is the meaning of "imminence" as defined by pretribulation rapturists?

Consider the following biblical facts in light of imminence:

> Could the Lord's return have been imminent before the gospel was preached "unto the uttermost part of the earth" (Acts. 1:8; cf. Mt. 28:19)?

Personal Observations, Notes, or Quotes:

Could the Lord's return have been imminent before Peter lived to be an old man (Jn. 21:18-19)?

Could the Lord's return have been imminent before the Temple was destroyed in 70 A.D. (Mt. 24:1-3)?

Could the Lord's return have been imminent before May 14, 1948, when the modern State of Israel was born, and there was finally a Jewish nation with whom the Antichrist could confirm or strengthen a covenant (Dan. 9:27)?

II. *Why This View Now?*

Read Chapter 19 of *The Prewrath Rapture of the Church* before answering the following questions.

Which of the systematized Rapture views can be said to be ancient with age? (p. 266)

Read the eschatological views (beliefs about prophecy) of the early church fathers in Appendix B. What did they believe concerning the Church and the persecution by the Antichrist?

Personal Observations, Notes, or Quotes:

Based upon this, which Rapture view(s) do you think they possibly would have held if the various Rapture views of today would have been systematized in their day? Why?

Which Rapture view(s) could they not have held?

If the prewrath Rapture view is in agreement with what the early church fathers believed, is *it* new or just *its systemization?*

What was the meaning of the command to "shut up the words" (Dan. 12:4)? (p. 269)

What was the significance of the second command to "seal the book" (Dan. 12:4)? (p. 269)

The Lord promised that knowledge and insight into prophetic truth would increase at the end of the age (Dan. 12:4). In light of that, should it be surprising that details of prophecy become clearer as we approach that day?

III. *Catalyst for Holy Living*

Read Chapter 20 of *The Prewrath Rapture of the Church* before answering the following questions.

Personal Observations, Notes, or Quotes:

A. *The Basis for True Hope*

What are the two distinct aspects of Christ's coming as it relates to the righteous and the wicked (Mal. 4:1-2)? (p. 279)

What should we exercise in discussions related to the timing of Christ's coming and the Rapture of the Church? (p. 280)

If pretribulation rapturism is not based upon clear biblical texts, what is it based on? (p. 280)

How does this compare to Dr. John F. Walvoord's view about pretribulationism and explicit statements in Scripture? (p. 160)

How does a prewrath Rapture become a catalyst for holy living? (p. 284)

What warnings does a pretribulation Rapture negate? (p. 284)

B. *The Seven Churches*

What do some believe concerning the seven churches of Asia Minor in relation to church history? (p. 287)

Personal Observations, Notes, or Quotes:

What are some of the problems of such a view? (p. 287)

What faithful action within each of the seven churches did Christ promise to reward (Rev. 2:7, 11, 17, 26; 3:5, 12, 21)?

What is the meaning of the word "overcome"? (p. 290)

During the Great Tribulation, by what do the saints overcome Satan and the Antichrist (Rev. 12:11)?

The Greek word for "overcome" (*nikao,* Strong's #3528) is later used for the saints in Heaven and is translated "gotten the victory over." What is it that they will "overcome" (Rev. 15:2)?

How did the Lord say that He would come unto these churches (Rev. 2:5, 16; 3:11, 20)?

Does it sound as if there may be thousands of years between the warning and His coming?

The Lord commended some of the churches for their patience (endurance under affliction – Rev. 2:2, 19; 3:10). In your earlier studies you found that believers will patiently endure affliction during what future time (Lk. 21:12-19; Rev. 13:10; 14:12)?

Personal Observations, Notes, or Quotes:

Christ warned the church of Thyatira that they would suffer what type of difficulty (Rev. 2:22)?

What future time period does this time of difficulty refer to in Scripture (Mt. 24:21; Mk. 13:19, 24; Rev. 7:14)?

How did the Lord describe His coming to the "dead" church of Sardis if they did not repent and watch (Rev. 3:3)?

How does this compare to Paul's warning of the coming Day of the Lord (1 Th. 5:2-6)?

Since the entire Book of Revelation is prophetic (Rev. 1:3; 22:18-19), it is only natural that Chapters 2 and 3 should contain a connection to that discussion. What conclusion might we draw concerning the Church's presence in Daniel's seventieth week in light of the following facts?

(1) The seven churches receive promises for being overcomers and, in a seventieth-week context, overcomers are later described.

(2) Christ warns these churches that His coming is very near.

(3) Christ commends certain of the churches for their patience, and patience is later defined in terms of the Great Tribulation.

(4) Christ warned the church of Thyatira that they would suffer great tribulation, and great tribulation elsewhere only refers to a time period inside Daniel's seventieth week.

Personal Observations, Notes, or Quotes:

(5) Christ describes His coming to the dead church in language like the Day of the Lord.

Personal Observations, Notes, or Quotes:

Summary

The following principles are taught by the Word of God concerning the return of Christ:

1. The Bible teaches that there is a still-future, seven-year period to occur. Within that period the Antichrist will arise, the Great Tribulation will occur, the Church will be raptured, and the Day of the Lord wrath will commence. That time frame is called the seventieth week of Daniel; never, the Tribulation.

2. The Bible teaches that there are three major sections to the seventieth week: the beginning of sorrows (Mt. 24:8), the Great Tribulation (Mt. 24:21), and the Day of the Lord (Mt. 24:30-31).

3. The Bible teaches that the Great Tribulation ("the time of Jacob's trouble") begins in the middle of that seven-year period but does not continue until its end. The Great Tribulation is cut short and followed by cosmic disturbance (Mt. 24:22, 29; Mk. 13:24-25).

4. The Bible teaches that Elijah (or one like him, if preferred) must appear before the Day of the Lord commences. If he appears before the seventieth week, there can be no pretribulational doctrine of imminence. If he appears after it begins, the Day of the Lord cannot start at the beginning of the seventieth week, as pretribulationism normally insists.

Personal Observations, Notes, or Quotes:

5. The Bible teaches that the apostasy and revealing of the man of sin must precede the Day of the Lord (2 Th. 2:1-4). The apostasy and revealing of the man of sin occur within the seventieth week. Therefore, the Day of the Lord cannot begin before the first five seals are broken, or at the beginning of the seventieth week.

6. The Bible teaches that a cosmic disturbance immediately precedes the Day of the Lord (Joel 2:31). The cosmic disturbance begins with the opening of the sixth seal. That occurs sometime within the second half of the seventieth week.

7. The Bible makes it clear when the Day of the Lord commences. There is no guesswork. It will commence with the opening of the seventh seal. John wrote, "For the great day of his wrath is come" (Rev. 6:17).

8. The Bible teaches that the Day of the Lord is a time of unprecedented judgment upon the whole earth. It will also be a time for purifying Israel.

9. The Bible teaches that there is only *one* second coming of Christ — not one for the Rapture of the Church at the beginning of seventieth week and another seven years later at its end, as pretribulationism sometimes contends.

10. The Bible teaches that the second coming of Christ (*parousia*) speaks of *a coming and continuous presence* to accomplish a number of divine purposes. It will begin with the Rapture and be followed by the Day of the Lord wrath and the Lord's literal return to the earth.

11. The Bible teaches that the *end,* or *the end of the age* is the time of the final harvest (Mt. 13:39). The final harvest is the time of separation between the righteous (wheat) and the unrighteous (weeds, or tares).

Personal Observations, Notes, or Quotes:

12. The Bible teaches that the Church is to remain on the earth until the *end* (Mt. 28:20). The *end* is always a reference to the end of the age (Mt. 13:39-40). The *end* occurs inside the seventieth week, not immediately prior to its beginning.

13. The Bible teaches that the *end* ("then shall the end come," Mt. 24:14) commences with the opening of the seventh seal. The righteous (the wheat) are raptured (harvested into God's barn), and then the unrighteous (the weeds) are judged (harvested and burned) during the Day of the Lord, concluding with Christ's physical return to the earth.

14. The Bible teaches that at Christ's return, a surviving remnant of Jews will be regathered to Israel and saved. God's covenant promise to Abraham, Isaac, and Jacob will be literally fulfilled (Rom. 11:25-26).

15. The Bible teaches that, in connection with Christ's return, the nations will be judged (Mt. 25:32) and Christ's millennial kingdom will be established.

Personal Observations, Notes, or Quotes:

Personal Observations, Notes, or Quotes:

Appendix A

Imminence: Does the Bible Teach an Any-Moment Rapture?

Almost two thousand years ago the Son of God left Heaven's glory and came to earth to become the Son of Man. He who had eternally existed with the Father and Spirit in perfect unbroken fellowship, took on human form and became a man. His miraculous birth, sinless life, substitutionary death, bodily resurrection, glorious ascension, and enthronement at the right hand of His Father are all brilliant facets related to the first coming of Christ.

The implications of that direct intervention of God in the affairs of men can neither be fully fathomed nor, with the greatest of oratory and literary skills, overstated by mortal man.

The Lord's first coming was the noon hour of at least 6000 years of human history. Astoundingly, but not surprisingly, as the Jewish prophets foretold, God was dwelling in human form among His creation. Men could see the visible Son and know precisely what the invisible Father was like, for Jesus was "the brightness of his glory, and the express image of his person" (Heb. 1:3).

Only one event, in the still-to-unfold future that awaits mankind, will be able to compare in significance with the first coming of the Son of Man. That event can be succinctly summed up in four words: Jesus is coming again.

Among the major purposes associated with the Second Coming will be the consummation of salvation for those who have died in Christ ("the dead in Christ shall rise first," 1 Th. 4:16); deliverance of the living who have trusted Christ as Savior ("Then we who are alive and remain shall be caught up together with them," 1 Th. 4:17); the judgment of the wicked during the Day of the Lord ("For yourselves know perfectly that the day of the Lord so cometh as a thief in the night. For when they shall say, Peace and safety, then sudden destruction cometh upon them, as travail upon a

Personal Observations, Notes, or Quotes:

woman with child, and they shall not escape," 1 Th. 5:2-3); and the establishment of Christ's rule over the earth ("The kingdom of this world is become the kingdom of our Lord, and of his Christ, and he shall reign forever and ever," Rev. 11:15).

The resurrection of the dead, the final redemption of the righteous living, the judgment of the wicked, and the introduction of a golden age, then, are major themes related to Christ's return.

Is the Return of Christ Imminent?

For those who believe and honor God's Word, the **fact** of the return of Christ to earth is beyond debate. Concerning that return, a significant number of Bible-believing Christians believe the Bible teaches that Christ's return will be premillennial — that is, at His return He will personally establish a literal, thousand-year kingdom on the earth. And, with that position, this writer strongly concurs.

However, there has been considerable, spirited debate with regard to the seven-year period (often referred to as the Tribulation Period or the seventieth week of Daniel) immediately preceding Christ's physical return to the earth and its relationship to the timing of the Rapture. Some contend that the Rapture of the Church will occur prior to the commencement of that seven-year period, or pretribulationally.

Intimately associated with the pretribulational view of the Rapture is the belief in *imminence*. ***Imminence*** is commonly expressed by the concept of an ***any-moment Rapture***. It is sometimes voiced with the sentiment, "I'm looking for the *upper Taker* (Christ), not the *undertaker* (the Antichrist)."

A number of Second Coming hymns suggest *imminence* in their lyrics. Leila Morris wrote,

Jesus is coming to earth again —
What if it were today?
Coming in power and love to reign —
What if it were today?
Coming to claim His chosen Bride,
All the redeemed and purified,
Over this whole earth scattered wide —
What if it were today?

And in the same vein, George Whitcomb wrote,

Jesus may come today —
Glad day! Glad day!
And I would see my Friend;
Dangers and troubles would end
If Jesus should come today.

Personal Observations, Notes, or Quotes:

Many outstanding seminaries, Bible colleges, missionary agencies, and churches include *imminence* in their doctrinal statement.

A large number of those who hold to a pretribulational and *imminent* return of Christ view *imminence* as an **important** doctrine, but not a **divisive** doctrine. They give genuine latitude to those holding divergent views on the chronology of the Second Coming. Others, however, have "set" pretribulational rapturism "in concrete," and in such circles to even raise genuine questions concerning *imminence* is to incur wrath and to be held suspect.

Amazingly, a doctrine which was virtually unknown in America 120 years ago has now become, for some, a fundamental of the faith. Of course, the bottom line — the final arbiter in every spiritual debate — is to be the Word of God; never tradition, church dogma, or human preferences.

The Origin and Early Definitions of Imminence

Some writers have attempted to anchor pretribulational rapturism and its handmaiden, *imminence*, in the rock of antiquity and the early church. It has been suggested that extant historical documents show that the early church believed in an any-moment pretribulational Rapture. In point of fact, quotations from the early church fathers suggest that (1) they believed that Christ could return in their lifetime, and (2) that His return would be preceded by a period of difficulty. But in no sense did they teach that the Rapture was pretribulational or *imminent*.

A review of Ante-Nicene writings overwhelmingly substantiates the reality of this statement. Neither the writings of Clement of Rome (30-100 A.D.), "The Epistle to Barnabas" (130 A.D.), "The Shepherd of Hermas" (150 A.D.), "The Didache" (150 A.D.), Ignatius (50-115 A.D.), Polycarp (70-167 A.D.), Papias (80-163 A.D.), Pothinus (87-177 A.D.), Justyn Martyr (100-168 A.D.), Melito of Sardis (100-170 A.D.), Hegisippus (130-190 A.D.), Tatian (130-190 A.D.), Irenaeus (140-202 A.D.), Tertullian (150-220 A.D.), Hippolytus (160-240 A.D.), Cyprian (200-258 A.D.), Commodian (200-270 A.D.), Nepos (230-280 A.D.), Coracion (230-280 A.D.), Victorinus (240-303 A.D.), Methodius (250-311 A.D.), or Lactantius (240-330 A.D.) lend support to the validity of a pretribulation rapture.[1]

John Sproule, writing in defense of pretribulational rapturism, nonetheless

Personal Observations, Notes, or Quotes:

with candor and integrity, noted concerning *imminency*:

> *. . . one of the recognized deans of pretrib. eschatology, refers to imminency as the heart of pretribulationism. Yet he is able to muster only a few vague quotations from the Early Church Fathers plus a few debatable scriptures (Jn. 14:1-3; 1 Th. 1:10, 13-18; 5:6; & 1 Cor. 1:7) to support his statement.*[2]

Sproule goes on to write:

> *Pretribulationism can ill afford to rest on the shaky foundation of traditionalism and eisegetical [reading into the text what is not there] statements. If its [i.e., pretribulationism's] "heart" is a debatable and inductively determined doctrine of imminency then, perhaps, an exegetical "heart transplant" may be in order.*[3]

Far from having its roots in the early church, pretribulational rapturism and an any-moment Rapture can trace its origin back to John Darby and the Plymouth Brethren in the year 1830. Some scholars, seeking to prove error by association, have attempted (perhaps unfairly) to trace its origin back two years earlier to a charismatic, visionary woman, named Margaret MacDonald.[4] In any case, neither its recent origin nor its source proves or disproves its correctness. But if pretribulational rapturism is used for a badge of fellowship and orthodoxy, one is faced with the perplexing question of what to do with the millions of godly believers who, for almost eighteen hundred years, did not hold to pretribulational rapturism. Among them are heroes of the faith like John Wesley, Charles Wesley, Charles Spurgeon, Matthew Henry, John Knox, John Huss, William Carey, John Calvin, Isaac Newton, George Whitfield, A. B. Simpson, George Mueller, John Newton, Jonathan Edwards, John Wycliffe, John Bunyan, and multitudes more. Would these men be spurned today because they were not pretribulational?

The pretribulational view of Christ's return made its way from England to America in the 1870s and with it, unfortunately, came friction and division. The Scofield Reference Bible (which has helped millions of people in their personal Bible study) made pretribulational teaching a major facet of its 1917 revised edition. Untold multitudes became pretribulational as a result of Scofield's notes which, because attached to his reference Bible, became highly authoritative in the minds of many.

It was the Niagara Bible Conference, however, which initially spearheaded the growth of pretribulational rapturism and the concept of an any-

Personal Observations, Notes, or Quotes:

moment Rapture in America. In 1878, the Conference adopted a 14-point doctrinal statement. The fourteenth section dealing with the return of Christ stated: "This personal and premillennial advent is the blessed hope set before us in the Gospel for which we should be constantly looking."[5] This was a broad statement which could be embraced by all premillenarians. However, later that same year, The First General American Bible and Prophetic Conference (closely aligned with the Niagara Conference) in New York City passed five resolutions. In Article 3, they went beyond the Niagara statement. Their resolution stated: "This second coming of the Lord is everywhere in the scriptures represented as imminent, and may occur at any moment.[6] Debate on the interpretation of the meaning of *imminence* followed. Some argued that *imminence* meant that signs **could** be fulfilled and that Christ could return within the lifetime of any individual generation of believers.[7] This view of *imminence* could better be described as ***expectancy***. It conveyed two facts: (1) Christ could return in any generation, and (2) signs could precede His coming. If the word "could" in point two (2) were changed to "will," their statement would reflect precisely the view of this article. A second group argued that *imminence* meant that the coming of Christ was possible at any hour.[8]

It was the position of this latter group which, in the years that followed, dominated pretribulational thinking.

With the passing of time, the definition of *imminence* was more closely defined. John R. Rice wrote:

> *Christ's coming is imminent. That means that Jesus may come at any moment. That means that there is no other prophesied event which must occur before Christ's coming. Nothing else needs to happen before Jesus may come. No signs need precede it. Jesus may come today.*[9]

Any moment — no prophesied event must occur — nothing else needs to happen — it could be today; these are the points Rice emphasizes.

John Sproule, in a context of taking issue with posttribulationalist Robert Gundry's definition of *imminence*, wrote:

> *More representative of the pretrib. concept of imminency is the belief that, without qualification, Christ can return for His Church at any moment and that no predicted event will intervene before that return.*[10]

In this definition, the emphasis is changed from *no prophesied event* ***must*** *occur* to *no prophesied event* ***will*** *intervene* before Christ's return.

Personal Observations, Notes, or Quotes:

It is one thing to speak of the Rapture as *imminent* and mean by that that Christ could come in one's lifetime and signs can precede that coming. It is another thing altogether to define *imminent* as meaning that Christ could return at any moment; that His return is signless, and that no prophecies will intervene before He returns.

Is Imminence a Biblical Doctrine?

It has already been noted that there is no historical evidence to demonstrate that the early church believed in an any-moment Rapture. (It should be added that that fact is in marked contrast to the overwhelming evidence that the early church was premillennial.) In fact, biblical statements preclude the early church from believing in *imminence*. The gospel had to be preached throughout the world before Christ could return (Acts 1:8). For the early church, that precluded an any-moment Rapture. Peter was to live to be an old man (Jn. 21:18-19). For the early church, that precluded an any-moment Rapture. The Temple was to be destroyed before Christ returned (Mt. 24:1-3). For the early church, that precluded an any-moment Rapture.

Some, attempting to circumvent this very real dilemma, have suggested that after those events were fulfilled the Church began to believe in *imminence*. Not only is there no valid evidence for that reasoning, but it continues to contradict Scripture.

Based on Daniel 9:27 and the prophet's words, "he shall confirm the covenant with many for one week," pretribulationists have historically and continuously insisted that the Antichrist will make a covenant with Israel to protect her for seven years (the seventieth week of the Book of Daniel). It is that event which triggers what is commonly referred to as the *Tribulation Period*. But from the defeat of the Jewish nation in 70 A.D. until the emergence of the modern State on May 14, 1948, no Jewish nation or representative government existed. Hal Lindsey has written:

> *The events leading up to the coming of the Messiah Jesus are strewn throughout the Old and New Testament prophets like pieces of a great jigsaw puzzle. The key piece of the puzzle which was missing until our time, was that Israel had to be back in her ancient homeland, reestablished as a nation. When this occurred in May 1948, the whole prophetic scenario began to fall together with dizzying speed.*[11]

Personal Observations, Notes, or Quotes:

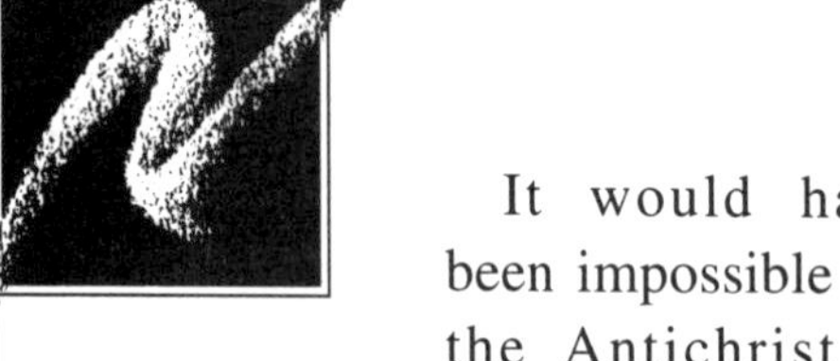

It would have been impossible for the Antichrist to sign a covenant of protection with a non-existent nation. An any-moment Rapture, therefore, was not possible before the modern State of Israel was resurrected out of the ashes of the Second World War. Israel could have become a nation during any generation — but the Rapture could not have preceded that event.

Above all other issues, the fact remains that there is not one verse of Scripture that teaches *imminence*, if by *imminence* it is meant that Christ's return is signless, any-moment, and without the possibility of fulfilled prophecies preceding it. The student of the Word will search in vain for exegetical evidence to support *imminency*. The fact that men are to "wait for," "expect," "look for," "keep awake," "be free from excess," "be alert," (and similar phrases) does not substantiate the claim that no prophesied event can occur before the Rapture. A chart listing verses that demonstrate that fact follows:

TEXT	BASIC MEANING (Greek)
Luke 12:36 Titus 2:13	Wait for, expect
Romans 8:23 Galatians 5:5 Hebrews 9:28	Await eagerly
James 5:7	Expect, wait for
Matthew 24:50 2 Peter 3:12-14	Wait for, look for, expect
1 Thessalonians 5:6, 8	Be sober, self-controlled
1 Peter 1:13; 4:7	Free from excess
Matthew 24:42-43 Revelation 16:15	To be awake, to keep awake
Mark 13:33 Hebrews 10:25	To see, look at
1 Thessalonians 1:10	To wait for, expect, near
Philippians 4:5 James 5:8-9	At hand

If church history and the New Testament do not support an any-moment, signless, no-prophesied-events-can-occur-first concept of the Rapture, from where did such a concept come,

Personal Observations, Notes, or Quotes:

and how did it grow to dominate much of the conservative Bible-believing, evangelical church?

Pretribulationists have rightly understood that the Book of Daniel provides the backbone of prophetic interpretation; that at the end of Daniel's sixty-ninth prophetic week the Messiah (Christ) would be cut off (Dan. 9:26). They also correctly understood that an indefinite period of time intervened between the sixty-ninth and seventieth week.[12] Coupled with that was the belief that Israel's prophetic time clock will again commence when the seventieth week is initiated with the signing of the covenant between the Antichrist and Israel. Of necessity, for pretribulationism to be correct, the Rapture **must** occur before God's prophetic time clock begins again with the seventieth week of Daniel. Pretribulationism requires a signless, any-moment, *imminent* Rapture of the Church. Without *imminence*, pretribulationism is dead. Or, put another way, if pretribulational rapturism could be exegetically proven, *imminence* would be demonstrated to be a logical corollary. *Imminence* would be a necessary outgrowth of a proven pretribulational Rapture, but **an unproven concept of *imminence* cannot be used to prove pretribulationism.** Here is a classic illustration of putting the cart before the horse, and it is routinely done in defense of pretribulational rapturism. The battle cry is sometimes voiced this way: *Christ can come for the Church at any moment. Prophetic signs cannot occur. Therefore, the Rapture must be pretribulational.*

Pretribulational rapturists, with few exceptions, believe that the Day of the Lord commences with the Rapture of the Church. The Scofield Reference Bible is typical of this position. It teaches that the Day of the Lord will commence with the translation (Rapture) of the Church.[13] However, since the Day of the Lord is a period of direct, divine wrath upon the earth (Isa. 2:12-21; Joel 1:15, 2:1-2, 10-11, 30-31; Zeph. 1:14-2:3; 1 Th. 5:2-4), and since Paul taught that believers are "not appointed . . . to wrath" (1 Th. 5:9), it is *convenient* for pretribulational rapturists to commence the Day of the Lord with the Rapture of the Church. Doing so, however, has created monumental problems for the belief in an any-moment, no-prophesied-event-can-occur-before-the-Rapture position. Because of space restrictions, a few of these problems can only be briefly mentioned.[14]

First: The Bible makes it clear that cosmic disturbance *must precede* the Day of the Lord. The prophet Joel wrote:

Personal Observations, Notes, or Quotes:

> *And I will show wonders in the heavens and in the earth: blood, and fire, and pillars of smoke. The sun shall be turned into darkness, and the moon into blood,* ***before*** *the great and the terrible day of the* L*ORD* *come (Joel 2:30-31. See also Isa. 13:9-11; Mt. 24:29-31; Acts 2:19-20; Rev. 6:12-17.)*

Second: There remains a word from the last of the Old Testament prophets concerning that future day. It is a message that holds out some hope. Before the Day of the Lord begins, God will send a messenger to call the nation of Israel to repentance. Malachi, God's spokesman about four hundred years before Christ, recorded:

> *Behold, I will send you Elijah, the prophet,* ***before*** *the coming of the great and terrible day of the* L*ORD*; *And he shall turn the heart of the fathers to the children, and the heart of the children to their fathers, lest I come and smite the earth with a curse (Mal. 4:5-6).*

Third: In the clearest possible way, the apostle Paul notes two events which *must precede* the Day of the Lord. There must be (1) the apostasy and (2) the revealing of the man of sin in the Temple of God. Paul wrote:

> *That ye be not soon shaken in mind, or be troubled, neither by spirit, nor by word, nor by letter as from us, as that the day of the Lord is present. Let no man deceive you by any means; for that day shall not come, except there come the falling away* ***first****, and that man of sin be revealed, the son of perdition, Who opposeth and exalteth himself above all that is called God, or that is worshiped, so that he, as God, sitteth in the temple of God, showing himself that he is God (2 Th. 2:2-4).*

The Word of God clearly teaches that cosmic disturbance must precede the Day of the Lord, that Elijah must appear before the Day of the Lord, and that the apostasy and revealing of the man of sin must occur before the Day of the Lord. Since pretribulationism states that the Day of the Lord starts at the Rapture, the concept of an any-moment, no prophesied-event-will-occur-first position is biblically impossible to sustain.

Expectancy, Not Imminency

Many believers within the early church had either seen Christ during His incarnation or known fellow-believers who had known Him. Consequently, Christ's life, death, burial, and resurrection were not

Personal Observations, Notes, or Quotes:

abstract issues of theology — they were vibrant realities. His promise of personal return was dominant in their thinking. Their Lord was coming again in power and glory. Things would be different when that occurred. God, not Rome, would be the victor. Christ, not the emperor, would reign. Righteousness, not wickedness, would be the order of the day. Unlike today, the heart of the Apostolic Age burned with the prospect of their Sovereign's return. They knew full well that the Church Age had commenced. The apostle Paul had revealed that fact (Eph. 3:4-6). But they had absolutely no concept of its duration. It is easy for believers in the twentieth century to look back at two thousand years of church history, but the first-century church had no basis for anticipating that kind of extended period of time between their own day and the return of Christ. They believed that their Savior could return in their lifetime, and their lives revolved around the expectation of that event.

That expectancy can be seen in Paul's first epistle to the Thessalonians. He wrote:

But I would not have you to be ignorant, brethren, concerning them who are asleep, that ye sorrow not, even as others who have no hope. For if we believe that Jesus died and rose again, even so them also who sleep in Jesus will God bring with him. For this we say unto you by the word of the Lord, that we who are alive and remain unto the coming of the Lord shall not precede them who are asleep (1 Th. 4:13-15).

With the use of the personal pronoun *we* in the phrase, "we who are alive and remain," Paul clearly includes himself among those who could be living at the time of Christ's return. In his second epistle to the Thessalonians, he emphasized the same truth. He wrote:

Now we beseech you, brethren, by the coming of our Lord Jesus Christ, and by our gathering together unto him, That ye be not soon shaken in mind, or be troubled, neither by spirit, nor by word, nor by letter as from us, as that the day of the Lord is present (2 Th. 2:1-2).

The adjective *our* in the phrase "our gathering together unto him" again demonstrates the apostle's expectancy of Christ's return.

A score of verses teach the Second Coming of Christ. All are consistent with the thesis that Christ could return in any generation. Among those verses are the following:

Looking for that blessed hope, and the glorious appearing of the great God and our Savior, Jesus Christ (Ti. 2:13).

Personal Observations, Notes, or Quotes:

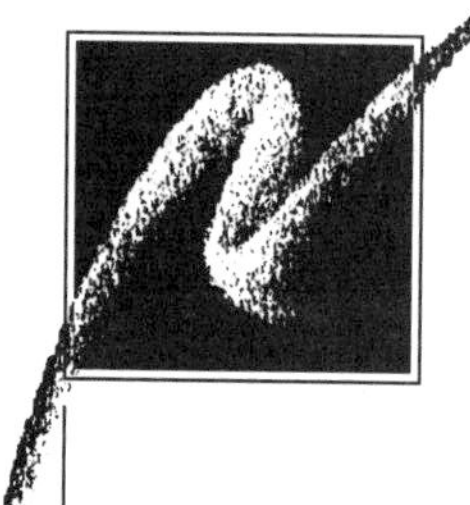

So that ye come behind in no gift, waiting for the coming of our Lord Jesus Christ (1 Cor. 1:7).

For our citizenship is in heaven, from which also we look for the Savior, the Lord Jesus Christ (Phil. 3:20).

So Christ was once offered to bear the sins of many; and unto them that look for him shall he appear the second time without sin unto salvation (Heb. 9:28).

And to wait for his Son from heaven, whom he raised from the dead, even Jesus, who delivered us from the wrath to come (1 Th. 1:10).

Expectancy — yes.
Imminency — no.

There simply are no verses in the Bible which teach that Christ's return can occur at any moment, is signless, and that no prophesied events will precede it — an absolute necessity to sustain pretribulation rapturism.

What the Word of God does teach is that every generation should be living with the expectation that Christ could return in its lifetime. That fact should be so real — that expectation so conspicuous — that it becomes a catalyst for holy living.

But, the generation which enters the seventieth week of Daniel will know that Christ's return is near. They will know precisely, because indicators will be given to that generation. The Lord taught, "Now learn a parable of the fig tree: When its branch is yet tender, and putteth forth leaves, ye know that summer is near" (Mt. 24:32). They did not know the hour or day when summer would begin, but they did know the general time period. For the Jewish person of the first century, the fig tree was a sign of approximation. When its branch became tender and put forth leaves, one knew that summer was getting close. That was a non-debatable fact. And then, using the parable, the Lord taught this truth: "So likewise ye, when ye shall see all these things, know that it [My return] is near, even at the doors" (Mt. 24:33).

The *things* that indicated that Christ's return was near had just been revealed by the Lord in Matthew 24:3-28 in answer to the disciples' question. They had asked, "And what shall be the sign of thy coming, and of the end of the age?" Those *things* are (1) the emergence of Antichrist, (2) war generated by the Antichrist, (3) famine as a direct result of the war, (4) pestilence because of the resultant unsanitary conditions, (5) martyrdom of some who will not submit to the mark of the Antichrist, and (6) cosmic disturbance. These events will indicate that the Rapture is near. Like the fig tree, they will be signs of Christ's

Personal Observations, Notes, or Quotes:

return. They will not indicate the precise hour or the day, but the general time period.

These signs of His coming cannot possibly have reference to Christ's physical return to the earth at the end of the seventieth week as some contend. That event will occur precisely three and one-half years (or 1,260 days) after the abomination of desolation occurs at the midpoint of the seventieth week. The precise day of His physical return will be known.

The coming of the Lord for His Church can best be described by the word *expectancy*. Jesus **can** come during any generation of history, but only those who are alive when the seventieth week of Daniel commences **will know** that the Lord's return is near. They will not know the hour or the day, but they will know the general time period because indicators will precede His coming. That is the significance of the Lord's teaching, "Verily I say unto you, This generation [the generation that enters the seventieth week] shall not pass, till all these things be fulfilled" (Mt. 24:34).

The Church Will Enter the Seventieth Week

God never exempts His children from the normal and natural difficulties of a sinful, unregenerate world. The destruction of Sodom was God's work — so He told Lot to get out of the city. The universal flood was His judgment — so He told Noah to get into the ark. The difficulties of the first part (the first six seals) of the seventieth week of Daniel are the result of the emergence of the Antichrist and the rebellion of unregenerate men against God. From those events the Church is not exempt. She will be exempted, however, and raptured before God's wrath commences with the opening of the seventh seal (Rev. 6:17; 8:1).

Therefore, it must be concluded that the Church has yet before her a period of great difficulty related to the activities of Antichrist before her final deliverance.[15] No normal person enjoys persecution, and the prospect of entering an unprecedentedly difficult period of time (the seventieth week of Daniel) is not a pleasant prospect. Understanding that fact should not cause God's people to recoil in fear and intimidation. It should be a call to holiness and preparation.

The Church is the Bride of Christ, and the Bridegroom would never harm His Bride. The Bible teaches that He does not — He raptures her before His wrath against the wicked commences.

The first part of the seventieth week is not the wrath of God. It is a period of time when the Antichrist will arise;

Personal Observations, Notes, or Quotes:

he will deceive many; he will enter the Temple erected for the glory of God; he will demand the worship from men that should be directed to the true Bridegroom alone. In that day, the true Bridegroom will be under attack. A false lover will seek to capture the hearts of men.

It would not be comely for the Bride to absent herself during such an hour of history. A true and courageous Bride will want to remain, fight, and give her life in martyrdom, if need be, to condemn the false lover and tell the world that Jesus Christ alone is the true Lover of her soul.

Nearing the end of His life and anticipating the approach and anguish of Calvary, the Lord asked three of His disciples to watch and pray with Him. They could have been of great help — an encouragement to the Savior in His time of need. However, when the Lord returned from His awesomely difficult time in the Garden of Gethsemane, He found His disciples asleep. The first Gospel records it this way: "And he cometh unto the disciples, and findeth them asleep and he saith unto Peter, What, could ye not watch with me one hour?" (Mt. 26:40). Gethsemane means *olive* press, for in that garden olives were squeezed to produce olive oil — and in that garden the Lamb of God was *squeezed* as he anticipated that which was before Him, and He "sweat . . . great drops of blood." He desired the support of His disciples in an hour of great need, but they did not give it.

During the seventieth week of Daniel, the Lord will need and want a courageous Bride to stand for Him and speak of His exquisite perfection as the gates of Hell are arrayed against His character through the Antichrist who will be directly empowered by Satan (Rev. 13:4). Will the Church, His Bride, be asleep, having been convinced of an any-moment, signless, *imminent* Rapture? Will she have become so complacent and worldly that her only concern will be her well-being and escape rather than the glory of the Bridegroom? Will she neglect the oft-repeated warnings to be ready, watching, and expectant?

The apostle Paul taught an important principle which the church in America would do well to be reminded of: "If we suffer, we shall also reign with him; if we deny him, he also will deny us" (2 Tim. 2:12). This could be the generation that will enter the seventieth week of Daniel. Some of us may be called upon to suffer even to the extent of martyrdom. If we are not willing to make such a sacrifice for our sovereign Lord, we are not deserving of being called His disciple.

Jesus is coming again. The dead in Christ will be raised, the living caught up — both to meet the Lord in the air

Personal Observations, Notes, or Quotes:

and be forever with Him. The true believer just can't lose — Jesus **is** coming again.

[1] William R. Kimball, *The Rapture* (Grand Rapids: Baker Book House, 1985), 20-21.

[2] John A. Sproule, *In Defense of Pretribulationism* (Winona Lake, IN: BMH Books, 1980), 18.

[3] Ibid., 23.

[4] Pretribulation traced to Margaret MacDonald. See Henry Hudson, *A Second Look at the Second Coming* (Massillon, OH: Calvary Chapel), 3.

[5] Ernest R. Sandeen, *The Roots of Fundamentalism: British and American Millenarianism* 1800-1930 (Chicago: University of Chicago Press, 1970), 276-77.

[6] Nathaniel West, "Introduction," *Premillennial Essays of the Prophetic Conference held in the Church of the Holy Trinity,* New York City, Oct. 30-Nov. 1, 1878, Ed. Nathaniel West (Chicago: Revell, 1879), 8.

[7] Samuel H. Kellog, "Christ's Coming — Is It Premillennial?" in *Premillennial Essays*, 57.

[8] William J. Erdman, *The Parousia of Christ a Period of Time; or, When Will the Church be Translated?* (Chicago: Gospel Publishing House, n.d.), 126.

[9] John R. Rice, *Christ is Coming — Signs or no Signs* (Murfreesboro, Tennessee: Sword of the Lord Publishers, 1945), 3.

[10] Sproule, *In Defense of Pretribulationism*, 12.

[11] Hal Lindsey, *The Promise* (New York: Bantam Books, 1984), 199.

[12] That fact can be demonstrated in that at the end of the sixty-ninth week Messiah would be cut off (Dan. 9:26). That occurred approximately 32 A.D., but the seventieth week (Seven-year period, or Tribulation) would not commence until after the destruction of the Temple in 70 A.D. Therefore, the seventieth week could not possibly immediately follow the conclusion of the sixty-ninth. There was, of necessity, a gap of 38 years which has now extended to more than nineteen hundred years.

[13] *The New Scofield Reference Bible*, C.I. Scofield, ed. (New York: Oxford University Press, 1967), 1372.

[14] For a fuller discussion, see the author's book, *The Prewrath Rapture of the Church*, published by Thomas Nelson, and found in most Christian bookstores.

[15] The apostle Paul taught that one evidence of God's righteousness during His Day of the Lord judgment of the wicked would be based on the wicked's persecution of the righteous during the seventieth week of Daniel (2 Th. 1:4-8).

Personal Observations, Notes, or Quotes:

Appendix B

Eschatology of the Early Church Fathers

Justin Martyr: "The man of apostasy [Antichrist] . . . shall venture to do unlawful deeds on the earth against us the Christians . . ." (*Dialogue with Trypho the Jew* 110).

The Pastor of Hermas: "Happy are ye who endure the great tribulation that is coming on . . . " (*Vision Second*).

"Those, therefore, who continue steadfast, and are put through the fire, will be purified by means of it . . . . Wherefore cease not speaking these things into the ears of the saints. This then is the type of the great tribulation that is yet to come" (*Vision Fourth*).

The Teaching of the Twelve Apostles: "Watch for your life's sake. Let not your lamps be quenched, nor your loins unloosed; but be ye ready, for ye know not the hour in which our Lord cometh . . . for the whole time of your faith will not profit you, if ye be not made perfect in the last time . . . then shall appear the world-deceiver as Son of God, and shall do signs and wonders . . . . Then shall the creation of men come into the fire of trial, and many shall be made to stumble and perish; but they that endure in their faith shall be saved from under the curse itself" (Chapter xvi).

Personal Observations, Notes, or Quotes:

Elsewhere Matthew 24:31 is twice quoted (a verse which, in context, occurs after the middle of Daniel's seventieth week) with the substitution of the word "Church" for "elect" (Chapters ix, x). This is especially significant since this verse is viewed as the Rapture by those who hold a prewrath Rapture view.

Irenaeus: "And they [the ten kings] shall . . . give their kingdom to the beast, and put the Church to flight" (*Against Heresies V,* 26, 1).

"But he [John] indicates the number of the name [Antichrist, 666] now, that when this man comes we may avoid him, being aware who he is" (*Against Heresies V,* 30, 4).

He also places the resurrection of the Church and the Old Testament saints after the revelation of the Antichrist (*Against Heresies V,* 34, 3; *V*, 35, 1).

Hippolytus: "Now concerning the tribulation of the persecution which is to fall upon the Church from the adversary [he has been speaking of the Antichrist and the Antichrist's persecution of the saints] . . . . That refers to the one thousand two hundred and threescore days [the last half of Daniel's seventieth week] during which the tyrant is to reign and persecute the Church" (*Treatise on Christ and Antichrist* 60, 61).

Melito of Sardis: "For with all his strength did the adversary assail us, even then giving a foretaste of his activity among us which is to be without restraint [referring to 2 Th. 2:7-8] . . ."

Tertullian: "Now the privilege of this favor [to go without dying at the Rapture] awaits those who shall at the coming of the Lord be found in the flesh [those who are still alive], and who shall, owing to the oppressions of the time of Antichrist, deserve by an instantaneous death [Tertullian's way of describing rapture], which is accomplished by a sudden change, to become qualified to join the rising saints [those who had already died in Christ]; as he writes to the Thessalonians" (*On the Resurrection of the Flesh* xli).

Personal Observations, Notes, or Quotes:

". . . That the beast Antichrist with his false prophet may wage war on the Church of God . . . . Since, then, the Scriptures both indicate the stages of the last times, and concentrate the harvest of the Christian hope in the very end of the world . . . . " (*On the Resurrection of the Flesh xxv;* cf. *Scorpiace* xii).

He equated the Rapture of the Church in 1 Thessalonians 4:13-18 (*Against Marcion* iii, 25) and the resurrection of the Church (*On the Resurrection of the Flesh* xxiv) with Christ's coming to destroy the Antichrist.

Cyprian, commenting on the tribulation in the Olivet Discourse: "With the exhortation of His foreseeing word, instructing, and teaching, and preparing, and strengthening the people of His Church for all endurance of things to come. . . ." (*Treatise VII*).

He later discussed the persecution of the Christians by the Antichrist (*Treatise XI*, 12).

Commodianus placed the resurrection of the Church after the appearance of Antichrist and his tribulation but before the Millennium (*Instructions* xliv, lxxx).

The Constitutions of the Holy Apostles: "And then shall appear the deceiver of the world, the enemy of the truth, the prince of lies, whom the Lord Jesus 'shall destroy with the spirit of His mouth, who takes away the wicked with His lips; and many shall be offended at Him. But they that endure to the end, the same shall be saved. And then shall appear the sign of the Son of man in heaven;' and afterwards shall be the voice of a trumpet by the archangel; and in that interval shall be the revival of those that were asleep. And then shall the Lord come, and all His saints with Him" (*Constitutions VII*, ii, xxxi, xxxii).

Victorinus: He speaks of Elias the prophet, who is the precursor of the times of Antichrist, for the restoration and establishment of churches from the great and intolerable persecution [followed by a lengthy discussion of the persecution of the Church by the Antichrist] (*Commentary on the Apocalypse VII*, 351 ff.).

Personal Observations, Notes, or Quotes:

Lactantius believed that the coming of the Lord to resurrect the righteous was to take place after the Great Tribulation (*Institutes VII*, xv-xxvii; cf. *Institutes IV*; and *Epitome* lxxi, lxxii).

The Ante-Nicene Fathers (those early church fathers up until the Nicene Council of 325 A.D.), some of whom had been taught by the apostles, held that the Church would see the persecution of Antichrist before the Rapture.

For further research, the above quotes may be verified in *The Ante-Nicene Fathers* by Alexander Robertson and James Donaldson, New York: Charles Scribner's Sons, 1908.

Personal Observations, Notes, or Quotes:

Scripture Index

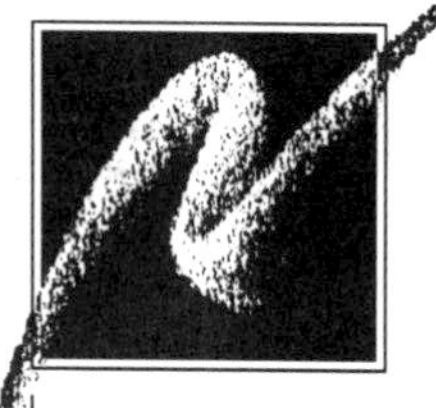

For Further Information

Many individuals, after completing this workbook, may wish to receive further information on available materials concerning Bible prophecy. Marv Rosenthal is presently the executive director of ***ZION'S*** *HOPE,* INC. (a faith mission to the Jewish people) and editor of *Zion's Fire*, a bimonthly, Bible-teaching magazine dealing with Israel and the prophetic Word.

For information on other available materials or for a one-year gift subscription to *Zion's Fire*, write: ***ZION'S*** *HOPE,* INC. P. O. Box 690909, Orlando, FL 32869; or call 1-800-4-ISRAEL (1-800-447-7235).

About the Authors

Born and raised in a conservative Jewish home, Marv Rosenthal placed his trust in Jesus as a teenager by following the example of his godly mother. After serving in the U.S. Marine Corps, Marv graduated from Philadelphia College of Bible and attended Dallas Theological Seminary for two years. He served in the pastorate for six years and for sixteen years was the director of The Friends of Israel Gospel Ministry, Inc., a worldwide missionary organization to the Jewish people. In that capacity he was editor of the magazine, *Israel My Glory.* Presently Marv is the executive director of ***ZION'S*** *HOPE,* INC. and editor of the magazine, *Zion's Fire*.

Marv is in great demand as a Bible conference speaker. His ministry has taken him throughout North America, to South America, India, Europe, and the Middle East on numerous occasions. Blending the unique combination of his Jewish heritage, his knowledge of Scripture, and his knowledge of the land of Israel, Marv is often invited to speak on the prophetic implications of current world events and the explosive Middle East.

Kevin Howard is a graduate of Cedarville College and is an ordained Baptist minister. He has unique insight into Jewish culture and the Hebrew language as a result of his involvement in the synagogue, the Jewish community, and his trips to Israel. Kevin served as an administrator and Bible teacher with The Friends of Israel Gospel Ministry, Inc. for more than six years. He is presently the business manager of ***ZION'S*** *HOPE,* INC. and is a frequent writer for the magazine, *Zion's Fire*.